simply grilling

simply grilling

Carol Heding Munson

SURREY BOOKS

Chicago

SIMPLY GRILLING
is published by Surrey Books, Inc.
230 E. Ohio St., Suite 120, Chicago, IL 60611

First Edition 1   2   3   4   5

This book is manufactured in the United States of America

Library of Congress Cataloging-in-Publication Data

Munson, Carol.

    Simply grilling / Carol Heding Munson.
      p. cm.
    ISBN 1-57284-026-9 (pbk.)
    1. Barbecue cookery. 2. Low-calorie diet—Recipes. 3. Low-fat diet—Recipes.
    4. Low-cholesterol diet—Recipes. 5. Salt-free diet—Recipes. I. Title.
    TX840.B3M86   1999
    641.5'784—dc21   99-17911
                       CIP

Illustrations © 1999 Patti Green
Editorial and production: Bookcrafters, Inc., Chicago
Design and typesetting: Joan Sommers Design, Chicago

For free catalog and prices on quantity purchases, contact Surrey Books at the address above

This title is distributed to the trade by Publishers Group West

A hearty thank you to Russell and Roger, who sampled and critiqued every recipe and enthusiastically offered opinions. And a loving thank you to Lowell for his generous contribution of creative recipes, his cheerful handling of the daily supermarket shuttle and his invaluable assistance with recipe testing. His encouragement and support made this book possible.

contents

introduction

I can't imagine not having a grill for cooking up fast, home-style food. My mom and dad had one: a simple round charcoal affair with a single round rack. Every Saturday and, sometimes, on Sunday, too, in warm weather, Dad would wheel it out, pour in some briquettes, heat things up, then cook a juicy steak or burgers. The meal was always simple. And we kids loved the smoky burgers that were topped with cheddar cheese, ketchup and pickle slices—and followed by marshmallow s'mores. We thought these were *the best* meals ever!

My husband and I bought our first grill decades ago: a teeny-tiny hibachi that we could squeeze onto a three-foot apartment balcony. Next, we graduated to a small round grill. It wasn't much bigger than the hibachi but it had legs. And legs meant we could dispense with a balancing act to grill on a railing or table corner. We used it until the bottom either rusted or burnt through—I can't recall which.

In my early days of grilling, our menus featured mostly traditional burgers and chicken with a commercial BBQ sauce. But as our family grew and the grills got bigger—and we switched from charcoal to a small gas version—we became more adventurous, trying fruits, fish, vegetables and combination dishes. (And we started grilling more often, from spring through fall, to be precise. Now, the only time we don't grill is when we're ankle deep in snow and the wind is blowing wet stuff in our faces.) We have whipped up speedy beef stir-fries, flavorful appetizers like shrimp cocktail, simple snacks (nachos are my favorite!), pizza and focaccia and decadent desserts (Amaretto Peaches makes a sensational sweet treat, especially for company!).

After years of grilling, I'd like to share my favorite fuss-free creations, the ones I serve often to family and friends. In this book, you'll discover more than 100 of my easy-to-make entrées, dinners and desserts such as Sirloin Loaves with Salsa Verde, Summer Shrimp Salad with Roasted Peppers, Lemon Chicken with Roasted Red Pepper Sauce, Lamb Patties Stuffed with Feta and Angel's Piña Colada Dessert. You'll also find a handful of delightful snacks and appetizers. For example, there are Mushroom

Caps with Gorgonzola Cheese, Crisp Nachos and Grilled Italian Bread with Sun-Dried Tomatoes.

But this book has more than fresh, simple recipes. To help you get the most from the recipes and your grill, I've put together a chapter on Grilling Basics and a table of Grilling Times plus a list of Emergency Replacements, a set of Kitchen Calculations (what equals what in the kitchen) and a glossary of more than 150 useful cooking terms.

I hope your mouth is now watering for a fast and fresh grilled dinner. Mine is (again!). Why not preheat the grill and cook up something new and tasty? Most meals featured here will be ready in less than 45 minutes. Here's to great grilling!

grilling basics

Getting Started

With anything we do, having the right equipment and accessories makes it easier, faster and more fun. Grilling is no exception. These are some of the useful options available (and you don't need to be a machine wiz to operate them!):

GRILLS

Charcoal grills: These widely available grills range in size from the small hibachi to the large kettle grill with a cover. Go for a hibachi if you live in an apartment with a small outdoor balcony or want something portable for picnics in the park. Requiring little charcoal, a hibachi has grill space for cooking burgers and chops for 2 to 3 people. Kettle grills, which are noticeably larger than a hibachi, come with lids—a neat feature that allows you to grill even when it's raining. What's more, foods grilled under cover cook more uniformly than those on an open grill. Select a kettle style if you plan to prepare more than one dish on the grill at a time or if you routinely cook for 4 or more people.

Gas grills: The heat source for these popular, easy-to-use grills is propane, and, depending on the model, it warms lava rocks, ceramic briquettes or metal flavor bars, which act as reusable substitutes for charcoal. Gas grills range from moderate size to quite large; prices go from around $100 to several thousand. All come with lids. My suggestion: Get a gas grill if you like the convenience of a quick start and simple clean up. Just remember, you'll lose the charcoal flavor. But there's an easy, smoky way around that. Simply place soaked hardwood chips or herb branches in a special "smoker box," an accessory sold by grill dealers. Check your owner's manual for directions. All the recipes in this book were tested on a gas grill but are appropriate for either gas, charcoal or electric.

Electric grills: Generally small, these are either stove-burner replacements or stand-alone units for countertops. Choose one if space is limited, if you want to grill indoors, or if, for some reason, you can't use charcoal or gas.

ACCESSORIES

Basting brush: Ideal for spreading sauces or "mops" over foods on the grill, these can be long-handled brushes especially designed for the grill, ordinary 2- to $2\frac{1}{2}$-inch paintbrushes from your local hardware store or pastry brushes with sliding ferrules for fast, effortless cleaning. Whichever you choose, make sure the bristles are heat resistant. My favorites are the inexpensive pastry brushes, which are small and easy to control.

Cleaning brush: These stiff—and usually made of brass—brushes aid in cleaning charred food bits from grill racks and other grill parts. Get one that follows your grill manufacturer's recommendations, especially if your model has porcelain-coated parts. Wire cleaning brushes are available in supermarkets and hardware and discount stores as well as from grill dealers. There's no need to spend a fortune on a brass brush, just get one large enough to take the hassle out of cleaning.

Fork: To grill large roasts or whole chickens, you'll need a sturdy fork or two for turning and removing the food from the grill. Get high quality, long-handled ones with two or three tines such as large chef's or carving fork. Grill forks with extra-long handles do exist, but I think they're a little unwieldy.

Gloves: Must-haves—no question about it. Get the best protective mitts you can, with plenty of padding and long wrists. Cooking on a grill is hot stuff.

Instant-read thermometer: This small inexpensive gadget is essential since there's no better way than using a thermometer for knowing when food—especially burgers, roasts and poultry—is done. Dial types cost about a third less than digital styles. But you can't go wrong with either one. Just remember to insert the thermometer near the end of cooking for a rapid read; do *not* leave it in during cooking.

Racks, baskets, woks, skillets: The rack that comes with your grill is just fine for cooking old standbys like steaks, burgers, hot dogs, anything that's too large to fall between the cracks. But for delicate foods, such as scallops, shrimp and vegetable pieces, you'll need something with small spaces between the grids. That's where the flat racks, hinged baskets, woks and skillets come in. They're designed for use atop your grill's standard rack, and they let you handle delicate fish fillets and bite-size pieces of food. Make your selection based on the type of foods you'll be grilling. For example, if you plan to cook whole fish, go for a basket with hinges. If you want to stir-fry, get a wok or skillet. For the recipes in this book, you'll find a flat rack and wok cover all your needs.

Skewers: Here, you have a choice between metal and bamboo. Either will serve you well. The bamboo versions are slim and disposable but must be soaked for 30 minutes before use. You can find them almost anywhere, including supermarkets. Metal skewers are thick, reusable and get very hot on the grill. These are best found wherever grill accessories are sold. I like the bamboo skewers because they can be inserted two at a time to keep foods from twirling around.

Spatula: Look for a sturdy one with a firm, fairly long handle and broad, flat blade. You'll need it for flipping burgers. For use on the grill, metal is a better choice than plastic.

Tongs: When it comes to turning small delicate items like chops, cherry tomatoes, asparagus, shrimp and mushrooms, tongs outperform the best forks. How's that? Tongs don't poke holes in food and allow juices to escape. For easiest manipulation, get spring-loaded tongs; stainless steel ones will last the longest. Choose those between 9 and 12 inches long.

GRILL FUELS

Charcoal briquettes: Readily available and widely used, briquettes come from smoldering wood. They may also contain binders and other chemicals such as starter fluid for quick ignition. If you use briquettes—a logical choice since they can be found almost anywhere, including supermarkets and discount stores—always heat them for at least 30 minutes to burn off the additives, which can impart off-flavors to foods.

Gas: Liquid propane (LP) or natural gas fuels gas grills. If you live in an area with natural gas, a line can be connected to your grill. Otherwise, buy LP in an approved tank, which can be refilled. Consider getting two tanks—one for use, one for backup—if you'll be grilling often. Replace the tank when it shows rust or other signs of wear.

Hardwoods: If you have access to hardwoods, feel free to use them for fueling your grill. Just remember to allow plenty of time for the wood to burn down to a white ash. Not sure whether a wood is hard or soft? Then don't use it. Softwoods produce a ton of sap, which makes harsh, unpleasant tasting smoke.

Lump hardwood charcoal: Often difficult to find (and sometimes expensive), lump charcoal produces a hot fire with delightful scented smoke. Use it in lieu of briquettes whenever you can find it.

Wood chips and herb branches: These add captivating flavors and aromas to grilled foods and can be used in both charcoal and gas grills. Simply add dampened chips to charcoal or place them in the "smoker box" of a gas grill. (Never use evergreens, pressure-treated lumber, painted or finished wood. All give off unwanted resins.) For guaranteed tantalizing results, pair up specific foods and woods or herbs. Here are some suggestions:

Alder: salmon, pork, chicken
Apple: ham, sausage, pork, fruit
Cherry: duck, chicken, turkey, lamb, fruit
Grapevine twigs: fish, poultry, vegetables, fruits
Hickory: pork, beef, poultry
Maple: ham, turkey, squash
Mesquite: pork, lamb, beef, swordfish, vegetables
Oak: beef, duck, pork
Pecan: poultry, pork, beef
Rosemary: fish, poultry
Sassafras: poultry, pork, seafood
Thyme: poultry, pork, beef

Cooking with Fire

In the following pages, I'll give grilling tips, including good ways to start charcoal fires, the difference between direct and indirect cooking, how to determine the heat of coals and preventing flare-ups.

FIRE UP

With a gas grill, starting up is as easy as opening the lid and igniting the gas. Follow the manufacturer's directions and preheat the grill for 5 to 10 minutes before cooking. (The first time you use the grill, you may need to preheat longer to temper the lava rocks and burn off any manufacturing residue.)

For a charcoal grill, pour in enough briquettes or lump charcoal to form a bed 2 to 3 inches deep and 2 inches beyond the area for cooking. Then light the charcoal by one of these methods:

Chemical starter: To use one of these starters, push charcoal into a pyramid, placing a solid starter at the base or soaking briquettes with a fluid starter. (*Never* add chemical starters after the fire is going.) Presoaked "self-igniting" briquettes need no additional chemicals. Place a lit match at the base of the pyramid and preheat for 30 minutes to burn off the oily chemicals.

Gas or electric starter: Use either of these instead of a match to ignite briquettes or lump charcoal. Both types are available in hardware and grill stores.

Chimney starter: To use one of these perforated metal cylinders, stuff the bottom with crumpled newspaper and fill the top with charcoal. Ignite the paper. The charcoal will ignite in about 20 minutes.

HOT DEFINITIONS

Generally speaking, coals are ready to use when they appear ash gray in daylight or glowing red at night. You can then level the start-up pyramid and begin cooking. But how do you know if the heat is high enough? On a gas grill, you simply read the thermometer. But on a basic charcoal grill, some hands-on skills will give you a clue. This is what to do: Hold your hand, palm side down, over the coals at the same height as the food will cook. See how long you can hold it there (count the seconds).

Check the guide below for approximate temperatures:

Hot: 2 to 3 seconds (425° to 475°F); use to sear meat, poultry and firm fish

Medium-hot: 4 to 5 seconds (375° to 425°F); use to cook beef, pork, poultry and sturdy vegetables

Medium: 6 to 7 seconds (325° to 375°F); use to cook fruit, delicate vegetables, delicate seafood and poultry

Low: 8 to 10 seconds (275° to 325°F); use to warm breads

DIRECT OR INDIRECT?

Recipes in this and other grilling books often refer to cooking over direct or indirect heat. What's the difference and when should you use which? The answers follow.

For direct grilling on either a charcoal or gas grill, place the food to be cooked on the rack directly over the coals. Leave the grill lid open. (Note: Some gas grill manufacturers recommend closing the lid.) This is the traditional method for quickly cooking steaks, burgers and fish.

For indirect grilling on a charcoal grill, place a disposable drip pan in the center of the charcoal and arrange hot coals around it. Place the food to be cooked over the pan. Close the grill lid. This method is best for grilling roasts, whole poultry and ribs, which must be cooked more slowly than steaks and burgers. Also use this method when basting with sauces or marinades or painting on glazes, which will drip and cause flare-ups.

For indirect grilling on a gas grill, place the food to be cooked over a burner that has been turned off (usually a center burner in a grill with three units). Leave the other one or two burners on. Close the grill lid. Most recipes in this book use this method. Why? Because it's fairly easy to control the heat, there are few flare-ups and the food cooks evenly.

With both direct and indirect cooking, always preheat the grill.

FLARE-UPS

There are two reasons for most flare-ups: too much fat and too much heat. By reducing one or both causes, you can lessen (and maybe even eliminate) flare-ups. Here's what to do:

Lower the heat: You can quickly accomplish this in several ways. On a charcoal grill, lower the lid, raise the rack, spread the coals, remove some coals. On a gas grill, simply turn down the heat. You can also remove the food and mist the coals or lava rocks (or flavor bars) with water. When flaring stops, return the food to the grill.

Choose lean foods: Select lean cuts of meat and trim excess fat from meat and poultry destined for the grill. Apply oily or sugary marinades, sauces or glazes near the end of cooking. Use indirect heat.

Cook on a clean grill. Clean the inside of the grill occasionally to remove built-up grease.

Flavor-Ups

A dash of spice. . . a few herbs. . . a simple soak in a nippy marinade. . . a splash of tangy-sweet barbecue sauce. . . a coating of fruity glaze—all such enhancements build tantalizing flavor in grilled foods. They also tenderize meats, poultry and seafood, say some grill aficionados. But when do you use a spicy rub? Or an acidic marinade? Or a sugary glaze? The choice is entirely personal. So read on. See what's what, then make up your own mind.

GLAZES

Usually made with a base of honey, preserves, ketchup or sugar, glazes add flavor to meat, poultry and vegetables and aid in browning. They may also add to juiciness and tenderness.

Quick flavor: Store-bought peach or raspberry preserves or apple jelly make tasty spur-of-the-minute glazes.

Technique: Because of their high sugar content, glazes burn easily. To reduce burning, brush them on during the last 5 to 10 minutes of cooking.

MARINADES

These simple concoctions, in which meats, poultry or seafood soak anywhere from 15 minutes to 8 hours, contain seasonings (often garlic, onions, herbs or spices) and an acidic liquid, such as wine, vinegar, yogurt or lemon juice. During the soak, the marinade infuses scrumptious flavor and may also tenderize the food.

Quick flavor: A commercially prepared vinaigrette-style salad dressing makes an easy rush-hour marinade.

Technique: Beef, pork and lamb can withstand marinating for up to 8 hours; poultry, for up to 4 hours; and seafood, for up to 1 hour. Longer times will result in a mushy texture. Always use a nonmetal bowl (or sturdy food-grade plastic bag) for marinating; the acidic marinade may pit metal containers and cause off-flavors. When marinating for longer than 10 minutes, place the food in a covered bowl in the refrigerator. If the marinade will double as a basting sauce, boil it for 10 to 15 minutes (after draining it from the meat, poultry or fish) before brushing it over the food. Oil or sugar in the marinade can cause flare-ups, so baste toward the end of cooking. Discard leftover marinade.

MOPS

A mop is really a basting sauce with a catchy name, the term coming from the small cotton mop (available from restaurant supply stores) that is used for brushing on the sauce. Mops may or may not contain sugar or ketchup.

Quick flavor: Any flavorful liquid can serve as an emergency mop.

Technique: Keep mops (the sauces) warm so they don't chill the food when applied. And don't swab them on too often; opening the grill delays cooking. If the mop contains oil or sugar, which tends to cause flare-ups and burn, brush it on near the end of cooking. Thoroughly wash the mop utensil after grilling and discard leftover sauce.

SAUCES

The sauces used in grilling range from something as simple as warm beer to a store-bought, hickory-flavored barbecue sauce. Almost anything goes.

Quick flavor: As with mops, any flavorful liquid can become a delightful basting sauce.

Technique: Brush on warm liquids; cool ones will chill the cooking food. And limit the number of times they're applied; opening the grill slows cooking. If the sauce contains oil, sugar or ketchup, which tends to cause flare-ups and burn, brush it on near the end of cooking. Carefully wash the brush after grilling and discard leftover sauce.

RUBS

Simple mixtures of dried spices and herbs, rubs are spread or "rubbed" over the exterior of meat, poultry or seafood before grilling. Rubs provide intense, intriguing flavor.

Flavor tip: Seasoning blends, such as Thai seasoning, Cajun seasoning and Italian herb seasoning, make fast, tantalizing rubs.

Technique: Apply most rubs in generous amounts. And, for max flavor, allow "rubbed" foods to stand for 20 to 30 minutes before grilling. If desired, rubbed beef or pork can be refrigerated, covered, for up to 2 days.

An Inexact Science

To be sure, grilling is an imprecise science. And the cooking times listed in this or any other cookbook are mere approximations or guidelines, not unchangeable rules. At least six things influence cooking times:

- grill design
- height of the grill rack from the coals
- heating material (charcoal briquettes, lump charcoal, gas burner type and number of gas burners)
- number of times the grill's lid is opened
- wind
- outside temperature

So, feel free to adapt suggested times as necessary to achieve appropriate doneness. And keep in mind that it's always best to err on the side of underdone. When needed, you can quickly and easily return food to the grill for more cooking.

Grill Safety

Because of its open flame, high heat and tendency to flare up, a grill must be used with caution. A few safety tips follow.

- Place the grill in an open area, away from dry leaves or other combustibles.
- Do not use gasoline or other flammable liquids near a grill.
- Keep children away from the grill.
- Have a fire extinguisher, bucket of sand or source of water nearby.
- Do not wear loose or flowing clothing that can catch the flames.
- Do not move a lit grill.
- Check the coals frequently until they are completely extinguished.
- Turn off gas at the source.

About the Nutritional Information

For the readers keeping an eye on calories, grams of fat and milligrams of sodium, I've included a nutritional analysis of each recipe in this book. The analyses were calculated using Nutritionist IV by First Data Bank. Please remember that all such analyses are close approximations. To get exact analyses, you'd have to send *your* dinners, each one of them, to a laboratory for complete chemical breakdowns.

This is what to remember as you read the nutritional information: Each analysis was figured for a single serving. If you eat a larger or smaller portion, though, you'll be taking in proportionally more or less calories, fat, sodium and fiber. Garnishes and optional ingredients were not included in the analyses, and, in most cases, would not have much impact on nutritional statistics. If an alternate ingredient is given or a range of amounts appears, the analysis was figured on the first item or smallest amount.

Refer often to the nutritional analyses that accompany the recipes. They'll help you—just as the "Nutritional Facts" labels on packages do—plan and prepare tasty meals that are good for you and that you and your family or soulmates will love.

mouth-watering meats

Apricot-Mustard Glazed Ham Slice

Country Ribs with Tomato-Marjoram Mop

Hot Kielbasa with Two Peppers

New York Strip Steaks with Ruby Port Sauce

Rosemary Lamb Chops with Baby Carrots

Sirloin Patties with Saucy Mushrooms

Sirloin with Lime-Beer Marinade

Sirloin Loaves with Salsa Verde

Thyme-Tied Pork Loin Roast

Veal Brochettes with Red Garlic Sauce

APRICOT-MUSTARD GLAZED HAM SLICE

After a busy day, it's time to treat yourself. And what could be better than an enticingly speedy entrée of succulent ham, like this one, with a sweet-spicy glaze that tastes as if you spent all day fussing? Accompany with easy grilled apricot halves and green sweet pepper rings.

- 1/4 cup apricot preserves
- 1 tablespoon ginger ale
- 2 tablespoons Dijon mustard
- 1/4 teaspoon ground ginger
- 3/4 pound center-cut, fully cooked, reduced-sodium ham
- 12 apricot halves
- 1 red sweet pepper, cut into 8 rings

Preheat the grill. Coat a grill rack with cooking spray; place on the grill. Coat a grill basket or topper with cooking spray.

Mix the apricot preserves, ginger ale, mustard and ginger in a small microwave-safe bowl. Microwave on Medium heat until the preserves melt, about 10 seconds. Stir to mix well.

Arrange the ham on the grill rack. Grill over direct medium heat for 8 minutes. Spoon the apricot-mustard mixture over the ham; turn with a spatula. Grill until hot through-out, about 8 minutes, spooning on the glaze 2 or 3 times.

Arrange the apricots and peppers in the grill basket. During the last 5 minutes of cook-ing the ham, place the basket on the grill rack. Grill for 3 minutes; turn with tongs. Grill until hot, about 3 minutes, spooning the glaze over the apricots and peppers once.

HELPFUL HINT

Cut slits in the edge of the ham to reduce curling as it cooks.

PREPARATION TIME:
10 minutes
COOKING TIME:
20 minutes
SERVINGS: *4*

PER SERVING:
Calories: 238
Fat (g): 7.4
Saturated Fat (g): 2.3
Cholesterol (mg): 49
Carbohydrates (g): 23
Sodium (mg): 871
Dietary Fiber (g): 1.9

COUNTRY RIBS WITH TOMATO-MARJORAM MOP

From Kansas to the Carolinas, recipes for traditional rib rubs and barbecue mops are closely guarded "state secrets." So for those without direct access to the "pits," I've created this extra-easy knock-off. It's winningly tasty; even the pros won't guess it starts with a store-bought sauce. Remember, this version is for a modest slab of succulent ribs—just enough for a party of four. Double or triple the recipe to go whole hog for a small crowd.

PREPARATION TIME:

10 minutes

COOKING TIME:

1 hour

SERVINGS: *4*

¹/₄	cup tomato barbecue sauce
1	tablespoon red wine vinegar
¹/₄	teaspoon freshly ground black pepper
¹/₂	teaspoon dried marjoram leaves
2	pounds country-style spare ribs

Preheat the grill. Coat a grill rack with cooking spray; place on the grill. Whisk the barbecue sauce, wine vinegar, pepper and marjoram in a small bowl until well combined. Arrange the ribs in a single layer on the rack. Coat with the tomato-vinegar mixture.

Grill over indirect medium heat until done, about 1 hour, turning once and brushing often with the tomato-vinegar mixture.

PER SERVING:
Calories: 228
Fat (g): 11.7
Saturated Fat (g): 4
Cholesterol (mg): 53
Carbohydrates (g): 4.9
Sodium (mg): 267
Dietary Fiber (g): 0.6

HOT KIELBASA WITH TWO PEPPERS

For sausage lovers, here's another scrumptious entrée from the grill: kielbasa (a favorite smoked Polish sausage, also called **kielbasy***) enhanced with roasted onions, jalapeños, cubanel and mushrooms. Serve with a side dish of pasta or garlic bread and a crisp tossed salad. Or tuck into a crusty roll.*

PREPARATION TIME:
20 minutes
COOKING TIME:
25 minutes
SERVINGS: **4**

2 tablespoons Polish-style mustard with horseradish
¼ cup dry white wine
¾ pound reduced-fat kielbasa
1 medium onion, thinly sliced
1 medium cubanel (frying pepper), cut into thin strips
3 jalapeños, seeded and cut into thin strips
8 ounces mushrooms, cut into ¼-inch slices

Preheat the grill and place a grill rack on the grill. Coat a grill wok, basket or topper with cooking spray. Whisk the mustard and white wine in a small bowl until well combined. Place 3 tablespoons of the mustard mixture in another small bowl and set aside for the vegetables.

Cut the kielbasa into 4 sections crosswise. Slice each in half lengthwise. Brush the mustard mixture over the pieces. Arrange in the wok or basket. Grill over direct medium heat until the sausage is hot throughout, about 20 minutes, turning with tongs once.

Toss the onion, cubanel, jalapeños, mushrooms and reserved mustard mixture in a large bowl. Transfer to the grill wok or basket. Grill for 5 minutes, tossing as in a stir-fry often.

HELPFUL HINT

Start cooking with a clean grill to help reduce the possibility of flare-ups.

PER SERVING:
Calories: 182
Fat (g): 4.4
Saturated Fat (g): 1.2
Cholesterol (mg): 40
Carbohydrates (g): 19.8
Sodium (mg): 594
Dietary Fiber (g): 2.5

NEW YORK STRIP STEAKS WITH RUBY PORT SAUCE

Use your favorite steak sauce and ruby port to create this singular sauce in which portobello mushrooms soak up the rich mellow port (a sweet fortified wine) and fresh chives contribute texture and bright color. For a complete meal, serve with roasted corn on the cob and a salad of mesclun, cherry tomatoes and cauliflower tossed with a bleu cheese dressing.

PREPARATION TIME:

10 minutes

COOKING TIME:

20 minutes

SERVINGS: **4**

1/3	cup minced portobello mushrooms
2	tablespoons chopped fresh chives
1 1/2	teaspoons whipped butter
2	tablespoons steak sauce
2	tablespoons ruby port
1	tablespoon water
1	pound New York strip steaks, trimmed of fat
1	teaspoon olive oil

Preheat the grill. Coat a grill rack with cooking spray; place on the grill. Mix the mushrooms, chives, butter, steak sauce, ruby port and water in a small saucepan. Place on the side of the grill to gently heat.

Rub the strip steaks on both sides with the oil. Arrange on the grill rack. Grill over indirect medium heat for 10 minutes. Turn with tongs or a spatula. Grill until the steak is cooked through and registers at least 145°F on a meat thermometer. During the last 2 minutes of cooking, spoon some of the port sauce over the steak. Heat the remaining port sauce and serve with the steak.

HELPFUL HINT

Protect the handle of your saucepan by wrapping it in several layers of foil.

PER SERVING:
Calories: 260
Fat (g): 10
Saturated Fat (g): 3.9
Cholesterol (mg): 73
Carbohydrates (g): 4.3
Sodium (mg): 188
Dietary Fiber (g): 0.1

ROSEMARY LAMB CHOPS WITH BABY CARROTS

The distinctive marriage of rosemary and Dijon mustard always pleases. Here, I've used the combo in a quick-to-prepare paste on lean lamb chops, but it would zip up a sirloin beef steak just as nicely. A splash of lemon highlights the caramelized flavor in roasted carrots.

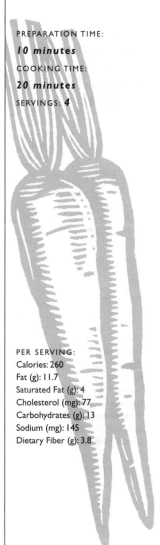

1½ tablespoons minced fresh rosemary
1½ tablespoons Dijon mustard
1½ teaspoons freshly ground black pepper
¾ pound loin lamb chops
1 pound baby carrots
1 tablespoon lemon juice
1 tablespoon minced fresh parsley

Preheat the grill and place a grill rack on the grill. Coat a grill basket or topper with cooking spray. Mix the rosemary, mustard and pepper in a small bowl until a paste forms. Spread over both sides of the chops. Arrange in the basket or topper.

Grill until lightly browned and cooked to the desired doneness, 15 to 20 minutes, turning with a spatula or tongs once.

Place the carrots in a microwave-safe bowl; add 2 tablespoons water. Microwave, covered, for 5 minutes; drain. Transfer to a grill basket. Grill until lightly browned and tender, about 10 minutes, stirring with a spoon occasionally. Sprinkle the lemon juice and parsley over the carrots.

HELPFUL HINT

Test the carrots for doneness often; overcooked, they're dry and leatherlike.

PREPARATION TIME:
10 minutes
COOKING TIME:
20 minutes
SERVINGS: **4**

PER SERVING:
Calories: 260
Fat (g): 11.7
Saturated Fat (g): 4
Cholesterol (mg): 77
Carbohydrates (g): 13
Sodium (mg): 145
Dietary Fiber (g): 3.8

19

SIRLOIN PATTIES WITH SAUCY MUSHROOMS

These steak-house-style patties put the sizzle back in weeknight dinners. That's because they're fast to make. They're flavor-packed with oniony shallots and fresh parsley. And they're juicy. Top the experience off with the rich portobello mushroom sauce. Perfect for a time-honored steak and potatoes meal.

PREPARATION TIME:
10 to 15 minutes

COOKING TIME:
25 minutes

SERVINGS: **4**

2	teaspoons olive oil
8	ounces portobello mushrooms, chopped
$^3/_4$	cup fat-free beef broth
1	tablespoon cornstarch
$^3/_4$	pound ground beef sirloin
$^3/_4$	cup rolled oats
$^1/_2$	cup finely chopped shallots
$^1/_2$	cup finely chopped fresh parsley
1	egg white
	Freshly ground black pepper

Warm the olive oil in a large skillet over medium-high heat for 1 minute. Add the mushrooms and sauté until lightly browned, about 3 minutes. Combine the beef broth and cornstarch in a measuring cup; whisk until blended and free of lumps. Pour slowly into the mushrooms, whisking constantly. Cook until slightly thickened, 1 to 2 minutes. Keep warm.

Preheat the grill. Coat a grill rack with cooking spray; place on the grill.

Combine the beef, oats, shallots, parsley and egg white in a large bowl; mix gently but thoroughly. Shape into 4 patties, each $3^1/_2$ to 4 inches in diameter. Arrange on the grill rack. Grill over medium indirect heat until done, 8 to 10 minutes per side, turning with a spatula once.

Top each serving with the mushroom mixture. Season with the pepper.

PER SERVING:
Calories: 284
Fat (g): 8.3
Saturated Fat (g): 2.4
Cholesterol (mg): 61
Carbohydrates (g): 20
Sodium (mg): 110
Dietary Fiber (g): 2.4

HELPFUL HINT

Fat-free egg substitute ($^1/_4$ cup) can be used instead of the egg white.

SIRLOIN WITH LIME-BEER MARINADE

Win high fives with this super-simple five-ingredient entrée. The available-anywhere ingredients? Beer (nonalcoholic may be used), garlic, lime juice, pepper and, of course, a high-quality steak. Allow 30 minutes to several hours for marinating.

PREPARATION TIME:
10 minutes plus marinating
COOKING TIME:
20 minutes
SERVINGS: **4**

- $\frac{1}{2}$ cup regular or nonalcoholic beer
- 1 teaspoon lime juice
- $\frac{1}{8}$ teaspoon garlic powder
- $\frac{3}{4}$ pound sirloin steak, trimmed of fat
- $\frac{1}{2}$ teaspoon freshly ground black pepper

Whisk the beer, lime juice and garlic in a small bowl until well combined. Place the sirloin in a self-sealing plastic bag and pour in the beer mixture, turning to coat well. Marinate in the refrigerator for 30 minutes to 8 hours.

Preheat the grill. Coat a grill rack with cooking spray; place on the grill. Rub the steak with the pepper. Arrange the sirloin on the grill rack. Grill over indirect medium heat until cooked to the desired doneness and the temperature registers at least 145°F on a meat thermometer, about 20 minutes, turning with a spatula or tongs once and brushing on the marinade once. Serve with fresh lime wedges if desired.

HELPFUL HINT

Make small slits around the edge of the steak so it doesn't curl while cooking.

PER SERVING:
Calories: 171
Fat (g): 4.8
Saturated Fat (g): 1.9
Cholesterol (mg): 61
Carbohydrates (g): 3.2
Sodium (mg): 58
Dietary Fiber (g): 0.6

SIRLOIN LOAVES WITH SALSA VERDE

There's elemental comfort in savoring old-fashioned, home-style meat loaf— especially this one with its smoky grilled flavor. Shape it into four loaves for easy handling and top it with salsa verde, a green Tex-Mex sauce made with tomatillos, in lieu of the usual tomato sauce. (Salsa verde is available in almost any supermarket.)

PREPARATION TIME:

20 minutes

COOKING TIME:

20 minutes

SERVINGS: **4**

1	pound ground sirloin
³/₄	cup soft rye bread crumbs
2	egg whites, lightly beaten
¹/₄	cup no-salt-added tomato paste
¹/₂	cup chopped scallions
¹/₃	cup minced fresh cilantro
¹/₂	teaspoon freshly ground black pepper
¹/₂	cup salsa verde

Preheat the grill. Coat a grill rack with cooking spray; place on the grill. Combine the ground sirloin, bread crumbs, egg whites, tomato paste, scallions, cilantro and pepper in a large bowl. Mix gently but thoroughly. Shape into 4 oblong meat loaves. Arrange on the grill rack.

Grill over indirect medium heat until cooked through and the temperature registers 160°F on a meat thermometer, 18 to 20 minutes, turning with a large spatula, once halfway through grilling. Spoon the salsa verde over the top of each loaf; grill for 2 minutes.

HELPFUL HINT

Form *firm* loaves so they don't fall apart during cooking.

PER SERVING:
Calories: 243
Fat (g): 6.7
Saturated Fat (g): 2.2
Cholesterol (mg): 75
Carbohydrates (g): 8.1
Sodium (mg): 391
Dietary Fiber (g): 2.1

THYME-TIED PORK LOIN ROAST

Lean pork is fit to be tied—not in anger but in generous bunches of aromatic thyme sprigs—in this recipe. During grilling, the thyme imparts captivating smoky flavors to a lemon pepper and yellow mustard rubbed loin roast. It's a dish fit for everyday fare and fit for a special feast as well.

PREPARATION TIME:

15 to 20 minutes

COOKING TIME:

1 hour

SERVINGS: **6**

- 1/4 teaspoon olive oil
- 1 pound center-cut pork loin roast
- 1 teaspoon lemon pepper
- 2 teaspoons yellow mustard seeds
- 3 to 4 bunches fresh thyme sprigs

Preheat the grill. Coat a grill rack with cooking spray; place on the grill. Rub the oil over all sides of the pork roast. Press in the lemon pepper and mustard seeds. Arrange the thyme sprigs around the roast and tie in place with kitchen string. Insert a meat thermometer. Place on the grill rack.

Grill over indirect medium heat until the thermometer registers 160°F, about 1 hour. Transfer to a platter and let rest for 2 to 3 minutes. Remove the thyme sprigs, reserving a few roasted leaves to sprinkle over the roast. Slice and serve.

HELPFUL HINTS

The thyme sprigs will char during cooking. Not to worry. The pork will remain succulent–juicy and tender.

Substitute a tenderloin for the loin roast if you wish.

PER SERVING:
Calories: 196
Fat (g): 9.8
Saturated Fat (g): 3.1
Cholesterol (mg): 47
Carbohydrates (g): 3.2
Sodium (mg): 108
Dietary Fiber (g): 0.2

VEAL BROCHETTES WITH RED GARLIC SAUCE

Showcase superb (and pricey) veal medallions en brochettes—French for "on skewers"—with this assertive garlic-basil sauce. It's a simple sauce but yields enticingly complex flavors. If veal isn't available, try the sauce with skewered pork or chicken.

PREPARATION TIME:

15 minutes

COOKING TIME:

30 minutes

SERVINGS: *4*

4 cloves garlic, crushed

2 tablespoons tomato paste

$1/4$ cup dry red wine

8 fresh basil leaves, minced (about 2 tablespoons)

Juice of 1 lemon

2 teaspoons sugar

2 teaspoons olive oil

1 pound veal shoulder, cut into 2-inch medallions

Olive oil cooking spray

Soak 8 bamboo skewers in water to cover in a shallow baking dish for 30 minutes. Preheat the grill. Coat a grill rack with cooking spray; place on the grill.

Whisk the garlic, tomato paste, red wine, basil, lemon juice, sugar and olive oil in a small saucepan. Pour $1/2$ of the mixture into another small saucepan and reserve for serving.

Thread the veal onto the skewers. Mist with the cooking spray. Arrange on the grill rack. Grill over indirect medium heat until done, 20 to 30 minutes, turning once and basting often with the garlic-basil mixture.

During the last 2 minutes of cooking, warm the reserved garlic-basil mixture for serving with the brochettes.

PER SERVING:
Calories: 162
Fat (g): 6.3
Saturated Fat (g): 1.9
Cholesterol (mg): 74
Carbohydrates (g): 5.4
Sodium (mg): 64
Dietary Fiber (g): 0.4

HELPFUL HINT

The reserved garlic-basil mixture can be warmed on the grill. Be sure to cover the saucepan's handle with several layers of foil to protect it from too much heat.

so
flavorful
fish

Albacore with Shallot-Caper Sauce

Bangkok Shrimp with Water Chestnuts

Blacktip Shark with Tropical Salsa

Grilled Shrimp Cocktail

Lemon Flounder on a Bed of Chives

Mandarin Tilapia with Summer Salsa

Red-Rubbed Catfish with Yukon-Gold Potatoes

Sea Bass with Sherried Mushrooms

Sesame Salmon Fillet with Potatoes

Shellfish and Feather Kabobs with Orange

Summer Shrimp Salad with Roasted Peppers

so flavorful fish

ALBACORE WITH SHALLOT-CAPER SAUCE

Tuna goes gourmet. Grilled and sauced with fortified wine and lightly sautéed shallots, albacore—aka white meat tuna—makes for an impressive, upscale dish. But don't wait for company. Serve it often—any weeknight will do.

PREPARATION TIME:

5 minutes

COOKING TIME:

15 to 20 minutes

SERVINGS: *4*

1	pound albacore tuna steaks
	Olive oil cooking spray
$1/4$	teaspoon white pepper
2	teaspoons butter
2	shallots, minced
$1/2$	cup sweet Marsala
1	tablespoon capers, rinsed and drained
8	fresh mint leaves (garnish)

Preheat the grill. Coat a grill rack with cooking spray; place on the grill. Mist both sides of the tuna with the cooking spray. Rub the pepper over the tuna. Arrange on the grill rack. Grill over indirect medium heat until cooked through, 16 to 18 minutes, turning with a spatula or tongs once. Transfer to a serving platter.

During the last 5 minutes of cooking, melt the butter in a small saucepan over medium-high heat. Add the shallots and sauté until golden, stirring occasionally. Stir in the Marsala and capers. Drizzle over the tuna; garnish with the mint.

HELPFUL HINT

Prepare the sauce on either the stove top or grill. If using the grill, select a saucepan with a heat-proof handle or protect a sensitive handle by wrapping it in several layers of foil.

PER SERVING:
Calories: 216
Fat (g): 3.4
Saturated Fat (g): 1.6
Cholesterol (mg): 71
Carbohydrates (g): 5.1
Sodium (mg): 158
Dietary Fiber (g): 0

BANGKOK SHRIMP WITH WATER CHESTNUTS

Be bold. Enliven large tiger shrimp with Thai seasoning—a zippy blend of chili pepper, ginger and 9 other seasonings—and forgo the oft-used garlic and parsley combo. Thai seasoning is available in almost any large supermarket, but if you can't find it, substitute equal quantities of cayenne, ginger, garlic powder and grated orange peel.

PREPARATION TIME:

20 minutes plus
10 minutes marinating

COOKING TIME:

8 to 12 minutes

SERVINGS: **4**

- 2 teaspoons peanut oil
- 1/2 cup rice wine vinegar
- 2 tablespoons reduced-sodium soy sauce
- 1 teaspoon Thai seasoning
- 2 cloves garlic, crushed
- 1 pound large shrimp, peeled and deveined
- 2 red sweet peppers, cut into 1-inch strips
- 2 cans (8 ounces each) whole water chestnuts
  Lemon wedges

Preheat the grill and place a grill rack on the grill. Coat a grill basket or topper with cooking spray. Soak 8 bamboo skewers in water to cover in a shallow baking dish for 30 minutes.

Whisk the peanut oil, vinegar, soy sauce, Thai seasoning and garlic in a small bowl until well combined. Place the shrimp in a self-sealing plastic bag and pour in half the soy sauce mixture, turning to coat; reserve the remaining soy sauce mixture to use as a basting sauce. Let marinate for 10 minutes, turning once.

Remove the shrimp from the soy sauce mixture, discarding the mixture. Thread the shrimp and peppers onto the skewers. Arrange on the grill basket; arrange the water chestnuts on the basket. Grill over direct medium heat until the shrimp turns opaque, 8 to 12 minutes, brushing with the reserved soy sauce mixture and turning once. Serve with the lemon wedges.

HELPFUL HINT

Marinating the shrimp for up to 1 hour will intensify the spicy flavors.

PER SERVING:
Calories: 184
Fat (g): 4.5
Saturated Fat (g): 0.8
Cholesterol (mg): 172
Carbohydrates (g): 11
Sodium (mg): 442
Dietary Fiber (g): 1.7

BLACKTIP SHARK WITH TROPICAL SALSA

Prepare for exotic flavors and be refreshingly rewarded. Blacktip shark (a firm, fairly mild, meaty fish) grills up juicy and pairs beautifully with this easy, fresh salsa of sweet-tart mangoes and papayas. The dish is as attractive as it is delicious.

PREPARATION TIME:

15 minutes

COOKING TIME:

20 minutes

SERVINGS: *4*

1/2 cup thinly sliced scallions
1 mango, peeled and chopped (about 8 ounces)
1 papaya, peeled and chopped (about 8 ounces)
3 tablespoons pineapple juice
1 tablespoon white wine vinegar
Butter-flavored cooking spray
1 pound blacktip shark steaks
2 teaspoons jerk seasoning

For the tropical salsa, combine scallions, mango, papaya, pineapple juice and vinegar in a medium-size bowl; toss gently to combine. Cover and chill, in the refrigerator, until ready to serve.

Preheat the grill and place a grill rack on the grill. Coat a grill basket or topper with cooking spray. Mist both sides of the shark with the cooking spray; rub the jerk seasoning over both sides. Arrange in the grill basket. Grill over direct medium heat until done, 16 to 18 minutes, turning with a spatula until done.

Serve immediately with the mango-papaya salsa.

HELPFUL HINT

If blacktip shark is not available, this recipe will work just as well with mako shark or tuna steaks.

PER SERVING:
Calories: 314
Fat (g): 5.5
Saturated Fat (g): 1.1
Cholesterol (mg): 58
Carbohydrates (g): 41
Sodium (mg): 96
Dietary Fiber (g): 2.6

GRILLED SHRIMP COCKTAIL

There are good shrimp cocktail recipes. And there are outstanding ones. This one with its smoky succulent shrimp and zesty lime and horseradish-infused sauce ranks among the best. It's a snap to make, too. I'm sure you'll agree.

PREPARATION TIME:

5 minutes

COOKING TIME:

5 to 10 minutes

SERVINGS: **4**

$3/4$ cup chili sauce

Juice of 1 lime

2 teaspoons prepared horseradish

1 pound medium shrimp, peeled and deveined

2 teaspoons olive oil

2 tablespoons minced fresh parsley

4 wedges lime

Preheat the grill and place a grill rack on the grill. Coat a grill basket, topper or wok with cooking spray.

Whisk the chili sauce, lime juice and horseradish in a small bowl until well combined. Refrigerate, covered, until serving time.

Place the shrimp in a self-sealing plastic bag. Add the oil and parsley, turning to coat the shrimp. Arrange the shrimp on the grill basket. Grill over direct medium heat until cooked through and pink, 5 to 10 minutes, stirring or turning occasionally with a spoon or tongs. Serve with the chili sauce mixture and lime wedges.

HELPFUL HINT

If desired, you can thread the shrimp onto bamboo skewers that have been soaked in water for 30 minutes. Plan on 2 skewers per person. When grilling, turn the skewered shrimp once.

PER SERVING:
Calories: 203
Fat (g): 4.8
Saturated Fat (g): 1
Cholesterol (mg): 173
Carbohydrates (g): 16
Sodium (mg): 207
Dietary Fiber (g): 0.6

LEMON FLOUNDER ON A BED OF CHIVES

Cook thin, delicate flounder fillets—on a grill? Absolutely. Won't they fall through the cracks in the rack? Nope. That's because these fillets are grilled on a protective bed of fragrant chives. The technique is extra easy and produces a warm onionlike aroma as everything cooks. The resulting texture of the flounder is moist, tender and sure to please. Grated lemon peel adds sunny pizzazz.

3 to 4	bunches chives (about 3 ounces)
1	teaspoon olive oil
$\frac{1}{8}$	teaspoon white pepper
$1\frac{1}{2}$	teaspoons grated lemon peel
2	teaspoons chopped fresh chervil or $1\frac{1}{2}$ teaspoon dried
1	pound flounder fillets

Preheat the grill and place a grill rack on the grill. Coat a grill basket or topper with cooking spray. Rub the oil, white pepper, lemon peel and chervil over the flounder fillets. Spread the chives over the basket; arrange the flounder fillets in a single layer over the chives.

Grill over direct medium heat until the flounder is done and flakes easily when gently probed with a fork or tip of a sharp knife, 10 to 15 minutes.

HELPFUL HINT

Get enough chives to form a moderately thick bed under the flounder. And don't worry if some of the chives burn during cooking; that's part of the charm (besides, you'll discard most of them anyway).

PREPARATION TIME:
5 to 10 minutes
COOKING TIME:
10 to 15 minutes
SERVINGS: **4**

PER SERVING:
Calories: 150
Fat (g): 3
Saturated Fat (g): 0.6
Cholesterol (mg): 77
Carbohydrates (g): 1.2
Sodium (mg): 120
Dietary Fiber (g): 0.7

MANDARIN TILAPIA WITH SUMMER SALSA

Just what the grill meister ordered: tilapia, or Saint Peter's fish, coupled with an ultra-light salsa of luscious mandarin oranges, tiny cherry tomatoes and Triple Sec, an exuberant orange liqueur. Tilapia, a variety of perch, is farm-raised in the United States and is generally available in supermarkets.

PREPARATION TIME:

15 minutes

COOKING TIME:

10 to 15 minutes

SERVINGS: *4*

1   can (11 ounces) mandarin orange segments, drained
1/4   pound cherry tomatoes
1/4   cup snipped fresh chives
1/2   cucumber, peeled, seeded and cut into 1/4-inch cubes
2   tablespoons orange juice
2   teaspoons Triple Sec or orange liqueur
1   teaspoon cider vinegar
1   teaspoon olive oil
1/2   teaspoon freshly ground black pepper
1   pound tilapia fillet

For the summer salsa, combine the mandarin oranges, tomatoes, chives, cucumber, orange juice, Triple Sec, vinegar, 1/2 teaspoon oil and 1/4 teaspoon pepper in a small bowl, tossing gently until mixed. Chill, covered, in the refrigerator until ready to serve.

Preheat the grill. Coat a grill rack with cooking spray; place on the grill. Rub the remaining 1/2 teaspoon oil and 1/4 teaspoon pepper over the tilapia. Arrange on the grill rack. Grill over direct medium heat just until the fish is done, 8 to 12 minutes, turning with a spatula once. Serve with the salsa.

HELPFUL HINT

To seed a cucumber quickly and easily, first peel the cucumber. Then, cut off the ends and halve lengthwise. Stand 1 half on end and scrape with a sturdy spoon from top to bottom, removing the seeds. Repeat for the remaining half.

PER SERVING:
Calories: 174
Fat (g): 4.4
Saturated Fat (g): 0.2
Cholesterol (mg): 0
Carbohydrates (g): 13.1
Sodium (mg): 58
Dietary Fiber (g): 0.8

RED-RUBBED CATFISH WITH YUKON-GOLD POTATOES

Love the seasoning in chicken paprikash? Then give this intensely flavored fish dish a try. The catfish is generously coated with paprika, the ground aromatic red sweet pepper that's so familiar in paprikash dishes. Yukon-Gold potatoes with their fluffy, buttery texture take well to grilling, but if you can't find them, substitute russet, or Idaho, potatoes.

4	medium Yukon-Gold potatoes
1	tablespoon olive oil
3	tablespoons low-sodium vegetable juice
2	teaspoons minced fresh parsley
2	teaspoons snipped fresh chives
1	tablespoon paprika
$\frac{1}{2}$	teaspoon crushed red pepper flakes
$\frac{3}{4}$	pound catfish fillets

Soak 16 bamboo skewers in water to cover in a shallow baking dish for 30 minutes. Microwave the potatoes on High for 5 minutes or parboil them on the stove top for 10 minutes; cut into quarters.

Preheat the grill and place a grill rack on the grill. Coat a grill basket or topper with cooking spray. For the basting sauce, whisk the olive oil, vegetable juice, parsley and chives in a small bowl until well combined. Thread the potatoes on the skewers. Use 2 skewers at a time, placing them $\frac{1}{2}$ inch apart so the potatoes don't rotate. Brush with the parsley-chive sauce. Arrange on the basket or topper. Grill over direct medium heat until tender and golden, 8 to 12 minutes, turning occasionally and brushing with the sauce.

Combine the paprika and red pepper flakes in a small bowl, stirring until well mixed. Rub over both sides of the catfish. Arrange on the basket or topper. Grill over direct medium heat until done, 8 to 12 minutes.

HELPFUL HINT

Catfish fillets are fairly thin so turning them as they grill is unnecessary.

PREPARATION TIME:
15 minutes
COOKING TIME:
20 minutes
SERVINGS: *4*

PER SERVING:
Calories: 299
Fat (g): 10.3
Saturated Fat (g): 2.0
Cholesterol (mg): 40
Carbohydrates (g): 35.6
Sodium (mg): 57
Dietary Fiber (g): 3.5

SEA BASS WITH SHERRIED MUSHROOMS

This four-star entrée takes a minimalist approach to delicious dining. Mild sea bass is simply grilled, brushed with dry sherry, then topped with mushrooms that have been poached in sherry and melted butter. It's an elegant dish but delightfully speedy.

PREPARATION TIME:
10 minutes

COOKING TIME:
15 minutes

SERVINGS: *4*

1	pound sea bass steak
$^3/_4$	cup sherry
1	tablespoon butter
8	large white mushroom caps, thinly sliced
	Parsley sprigs (garnish)

Preheat the grill and place a grill rack on the grill. Coat a grill basket or topper with cooking spray. Arrange the sea bass on the grill. Grill over direct medium-low heat until done, 12 to 15 minutes, turning with a spatula once and brushing both sides with $^1/_4$ cup sherry.

When the bass is almost done (approximately the last 3 minutes of cooking), warm the butter and remaining $^1/_2$ cup sherry in a small saucepan over medium-low heat. Cook until the butter is melted, gently stirring occasionally. Add the mushrooms, stirring to mix; poach until the mushrooms are hot, about 3 minutes, stirring often. Serve over the bass; garnish with the parsley.

PER SERVING:
Calories: 211
Fat (g): 5.6
Saturated Fat (g): 2.5
Cholesterol (mg): 55
Carbohydrates (g): 6
Sodium (mg): 112
Dietary Fiber (g): 0.7

HELPFUL HINT

To wash fresh mushrooms, gently wipe them with a damp towel or *quickly* rinse them under cool water and pat dry. Never let them stand in water; they'll soak it up as easily as a sponge would. Unfortunately, excess water will dilute their wonderful earthy flavor.

SESAME SALMON FILLET WITH POTATOES

Here's a great way to jazz up grilled salmon: Splash on rich sesame oil, soy sauce and tangy lime juice. Sesame oil is available in most well-stocked supermarkets. But if you can't find it, sprinkle toasted sesame seeds over the salmon. Ready in short order, this entrée is sure to become a rush-hour favorite.

PREPARATION TIME:

10 minutes

COOKING TIME:

35 minutes

SERVINGS: **4**

½	teaspoon sesame oil
2	teaspoons reduced-sodium soy sauce
	Juice of 1 lime
1½	teaspoons sugar
1	tablespoon snipped fresh parsley
4	potatoes
1	pound salmon fillet

Whisk the sesame oil, soy sauce, lime juice, sugar and parsley in a small bowl until well combined. Set half the sesame mixture aside for serving over the potatoes after cooking.

Preheat the grill. Coat a grill rack with cooking spray; place on the grill. Microwave the potatoes on High just until tender, 8 to 10 minutes. Arrange on the grill and brush with sesame-lime baste. Grill over direct medium heat until tender and browned, about 15 minutes, turning with tongs and basting with the sesame mixture often.

Arrange the salmon, skin side down, on the grill rack. Grill over direct medium heat until done, 18 to 25 minutes, basting once after 15 minutes. Serve with the potatoes and spoon the reserved sesame-lime mixture over the salmon and potatoes.

HELPFUL HINTS

When completely cooked, the salmon's skin may stick to the grill. That's okay. Using a large spatula, carefully lift the flesh and transfer it to a platter. To remove the stuck skin, soak the grill rack, as soon as it's cool enough to handle, in a sinkful of hot soapy water.

To prepare this recipe with salmon steaks instead of the fillets, rub both sides of the steaks with the sesame-lime sauce before cooking. The sesame oil will help prevent sticking.

PER SERVING:
Calories: 280
Fat (g): 7.4
Saturated Fat (g): 1.5
Cholesterol (mg): 51
Carbohydrates (g): 25.9
Sodium (mg): 158
Dietary Fiber (g): 2.1

SHELLFISH AND FEATHER KABOBS WITH ORANGE

Here, surf and turf—traditionally a shrimp and steak combo—is revamped for a light, fresh taste. Enjoy sea scallops, shrimp and chicken all marinated in a perky orange and cilantro sauce. Grilled orange and onion wedges complete the feast.

PREPARATION TIME:

15 to 20 minutes plus marinating

COOKING TIME:

20 minutes

SERVINGS: *4*

PER SERVING:
Calories: 156
Fat (g): 2.5
Saturated Fat (g): 0.5
Cholesterol (mg): 62
Carbohydrates (g): 18.3
Sodium (mg): 135
Dietary Fiber (g): 2.8

1	teaspoon peanut oil
1/2	cup orange juice
1	tablespoon Worcestershire sauce
1	large clove garlic, pressed
1	mild chili, seeded and minced
1	tablespoon minced fresh cilantro
1/4	pound shrimp, peeled and deveined
1/4	pound sea scallops
1/4	pound skinless, boneless chicken, cut into 1-inch cubes
8	orange wedges (2 oranges)
8	onion wedges (2 small onions)

Soak 16 bamboo skewers in water to cover in a shallow baking dish for 30 minutes.

Combine the peanut oil, orange juice, Worcestershire sauce, garlic, chili and cilantro in a small bowl, stirring to mix well. Place the shrimp, scallops and chicken in a self-sealing plastic bag. Pour in the orange juice mixture, turning to coat well. Marinate in the refrigerator for 30 minutes.

Preheat the grill and place a grill rack on the grill. Coat a grill basket or topper with cooking spray. Thread the shrimp, scallops, chicken, oranges and onions on separate skewers. Arrange on the grill basket or topper. Grill over direct medium heat until done, 15 to 20 minutes, turning occasionally and brushing with the marinade frequently. The kabobs may cook at different rates. When done, transfer to a platter and keep hot under foil until the remaining kabobs are done.

HELPFUL HINT

If some of the scallops are exceptionally large, halve or quarter them to create uniform sizes, which will cook evenly.

SUMMER SHRIMP SALAD WITH ROASTED PEPPERS

Here's salad with an attitude—a fresh-flavor attitude. Savor lime-marinated shrimp; gently roasted green peppers; and cool, crisp cucumbers—all tossed with a captivating basil-lime vinaigrette. It's easy. It's speedy. It's delicious.

 2 tablespoons minced fresh basil leaves
   Juice of 4 limes (about $^2/_3$ cup)
 1 tablespoon olive oil
 4 cloves garlic, crushed
 1 pound large shrimp, peeled and deveined
 8 ounces farfalle (bow ties)
 2 medium green sweet peppers, halved lengthwise and seeded
 $^3/_4$ pound tomatoes, chopped
 $^1/_2$ medium cucumber, thinly sliced
 $^1/_4$ medium red onion, sliced into thin wedges

PREPARATION TIME:
20 minutes plus marinating
COOKING TIME:
10 to 15 minutes
SERVINGS: **6**

Whisk the basil, lime juice, oil and garlic in a small bowl until well combined. Divide in half; each portion should be about $^1/_3$ cup. Refrigerate 1 portion to use as a salad dressing for the cooked pasta and shrimp.

Place the shrimp in a self-sealing plastic bag; pour in $^1/_3$ cup lime-juice mixture, turning to coat. Marinate, in the refrigerator, for 30 minutes. Fill a large pot with water and bring to a boil over high heat. Add the farfalle and reduce the heat to medium. Cook, uncovered, according to package directions until al dente; drain.

Preheat the grill and place a grill rack on the grill. Coat a grill basket or topper with cooking spray. Arrange the shrimp and pepper halves on the grill. Grill until the shrimp turn pink and are cooked through, 7 to 10 minutes, turning with tongs once. Grill the peppers until the skins are charred, 7 to 10 minutes.

Transfer the peppers to a glass bowl and cover. Let steam for 5 to 10 minutes. Rub off and discard the charred skin. Chop the flesh into bite-size pieces. Combine the pasta, peppers, shrimp, tomatoes and cucumber in a large bowl, tossing gently to mix well. Pour the reserved lime-juice dressing over the pasta-shrimp combination. Toss gently to coat. Serve warm or chilled.

HELPFUL HINT

Shrimp are cooked when they turn pink, curl up and are no longer translucent.

PER SERVING:
Calories: 278
Fat (g): 4.5
Saturated Fat (g): 0.7
Cholesterol (mg): 115
Carbohydrates (g): 38.2
Sodium (mg): 122
Dietary Fiber (g): 2.6

vibrant
vegetables

Asparagus with Lemon Vinaigrette

Cajun Corn on the Cob

Colorful Rice Peppers

Grilled Asparagus and Tomato Salad

Maple-Walnut Acorn Squash

Mexican-Style Corn

Mushroom Caps with Gorgonzola Cheese

Parsley Potatoes

Roasted Potato Salad

Sausage-Stuffed Sweet Potatoes with Peanuts

Spinach-Stuffed Butternut Squash

Stuffed Eggplant

Tomatoes and Peppers with Parmesan Vinaigrette

Tomatoes Stuffed with Ditalini and Fontina

Zucchini with Basil and Garlic

v i b r a n t   v e g e t a b l e s

ASPARAGUS WITH LEMON VINAIGRETTE

It's no secret that tender, young asparagus takes beautifully to gentle steaming. But grilling? Definitely, yes. Grilling, just until tender, produces juicy sweet asparagus that will tickle the taste buds of the most avid aficionado. Here, a splash of lemon juice and olive oil further enhance flavor.

PREPARATION TIME:

5 minutes

COOKING TIME:

5 minutes

SERVINGS: **4**

 2   teaspoons olive oil
 2   teaspoons sugar
 ¾   teaspoon freshly ground black pepper
     Juice of 1 lemon
 1   pound asparagus

Whisk the oil, sugar, pepper and lemon juice in a small bowl until well combined.

Preheat the grill. Coat a grill rack with cooking spray; place on the grill. Arrange the asparagus spears crosswise on rack. Grill until lightly browned and tender, about 5 minutes, turning with tongs once.

Transfer to a serving platter and drizzle the lemon mixture over the asparagus. Serve at once.

HELPFUL HINT

Choose bright green asparagus spears with tightly closed tips. Wash thoroughly to remove sand hiding in the tips, and peel the stems if they seem woody.

PER SERVING:
Calories: 59
Fat (g): 2.9
Saturated Fat (g): 0.4
Cholesterol (mg): 0
Carbohydrates (g): 5.7
Sodium (mg): 15
Dietary Fiber (g): 1.4

CAJUN CORN ON THE COB

A generous dash of Cajun seasoning—three kinds of pepper plus paprika and, sometimes, other spices—enlivens roasted corn's naturally sweet taste. Use a heavier hand if firecracker hot is to your liking.

PREPARATION TIME:

15 minutes

COOKING TIME:

15 minutes

SERVINGS: *4*

4 ears corn with husks

2 teaspoons whipped butter, melted

1 tablespoon Cajun seasoning

4 teaspoons minced fresh parsley

Preheat the grill. Coat a grill rack with cooking spray; place on the grill. Soak the corn (husks on) in cold water for 10 minutes. Pull back the husks; remove and discard the silk. Rinse the kernels with cold water to remove stubborn silk.

Brush the butter over the kernels; sprinkle the Cajun seasoning and parsley over the kernels. Pull the husks up and around the cobs; fasten with kitchen string.

Arrange on the grill rack. Grill over direct medium heat for 5 minutes. Turn with tongs; grill until the corn is tender, 5 to 10 minutes, turning once or twice more. The husks will be charred in spots.

PER SERVING:
Calories: 77
Fat (g): 2.1
Saturated Fat (g): 1
Cholesterol (mg): 4
Carbohydrates (g): 15
Sodium (mg): 4
Dietary Fiber (g): 2.2

COLORFUL RICE PEPPERS

These sure-to-please stuffed peppers boast a riot of color: red, white, green, yellow. They pack a ton of great taste, too—thanks to scallions, sunflower seeds, thyme and basil. The recipe makes enough for a side as is; for a main dish, double the recipe.

PREPARATION TIME:
20 minutes
COOKING TIME:
10 to 15 minutes
SERVINGS: **4**

2	large red sweet peppers
1/2	cup cooked rice
1/2	cup corn
3/4	cup chopped scallions
1/2	cup shredded extra-sharp cheddar cheese
1/4	cup toasted sunflower seeds
1	teaspoon chopped fresh thyme
1	teaspoon chopped fresh basil
1/8	teaspoon cayenne (optional)
2	tablespoons nonfat sour cream

Preheat the grill. Coat a grill rack with cooking spray; place on the grill.

Cut the peppers in half lengthwise and remove the seeds and membranes. Combine the rice, corn, scallions, cheddar cheese and sunflower seeds in a medium-size bowl, tossing to mix. Season with the thyme, basil and cayenne. Toss to combine. Stir in the sour cream. Spoon into the pepper halves. Arrange on the grill rack.

Grill until hot throughout and the cheese has melted, about 10 to 12 minutes.

HELPFUL HINTS

To toast the sunflower seeds, spread them in a small nonstick skillet. Cook over medium-low heat until lightly browned, stirring or shaking the skillet often.

If using frozen corn, stir it in while it's still frozen.

This recipe can be assembled ahead and stored, covered, in the refrigerator for up to 1 day.

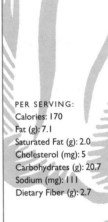

PER SERVING:
Calories: 170
Fat (g): 7.1
Saturated Fat (g): 2.0
Cholesterol (mg): 5
Carbohydrates (g): 20.7
Sodium (mg): 111
Dietary Fiber (g): 2.7

GRILLED ASPARAGUS AND TOMATO SALAD

Here's a warm toss-together that's high on freshness and low on fuss. Spring-fresh asparagus, juicy tomatoes and sweet onions are lightly grilled, drizzled with a basil-balsamic vinaigrette, tossed gently with mixed greens, such as radicchio, spinach and leaf lettuce. Serve anytime you crave a tossed greens salad.

PREPARATION TIME:
10 minutes
COOKING TIME:
5 minutes
SERVINGS: **4**

1	teaspoon olive oil
2	teaspoons sugar
1/4	cup balsamic vinegar
1	shallot, minced
2	tablespoons minced basil
12	spears asparagus
16	cherry tomatoes
4	slices onion
4	cups torn mixed salad greens such as leaf lettuce, radicchio, spinach, romaine lettuce

PER SERVING:
Calories: 87
Fat (g): 1.7
Saturated Fat (g): 0.2
Cholesterol (mg): 0
Carbohydrates (g): 16
Sodium (mg): 17
Dietary Fiber (g): 3.7

Whisk the oil, sugar, balsamic vinegar, shallot and basil in a small bowl until well blended. Preheat the grill and place a grill rack on the grill. Coat a grill basket or topper with cooking spray.

Arrange the asparagus, tomatoes and onions in the basket. Grill over direct low heat until lightly browned, about 5 minutes, turning with tongs once.

Transfer the vegetables to a working surface. Cut the asparagus into 1-inch pieces; break the onion slices into rings. Divide the greens among 4 salad bowls. Top with the asparagus, onion rings and tomatoes. Drizzle the basil vinaigrette over the vegetables.

HELPFUL HINT

For best results, the vegetables should be crisp-tender and *lightly* browned. Charring will detract from the delicate flavors.

MAPLE-WALNUT ACORN SQUASH

Sometimes, sweet is your ticket to dinnertime success. In this delightful side dish, maple syrup enhances acorn squash's natural sweetness. Walnuts add buttery crunch.

PREPARATION TIME:
5 minutes
COOKING TIME:
35 minutes
SERVINGS: **4**

1 medium to large acorn squash (about 2½ pounds)
  Butter-flavored cooking spray
2 tablespoons maple syrup
2 teaspoons grated orange peel
2 tablespoons finely ground walnuts

Preheat the grill. Coat a grill rack with cooking spray; place on the grill. Cut the squash in half and scoop out the seeds. Mist the cut edges with the cooking spray. Arrange, cut side down, on the grill rack.

Grill over indirect heat for 12 minutes. Turn, cut side up. Grill until the squash is tender, about 20 minutes. Cut the halves in half. Drizzle the maple syrup over the squash. Sprinkle the orange peel and walnuts over the syrup.

HELPFUL HINT

Generally speaking, acorn squash is in its prime in fall and winter.

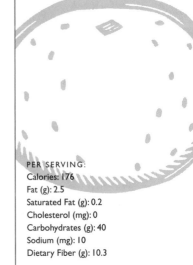

PER SERVING:
Calories: 176
Fat (g): 2.5
Saturated Fat (g): 0.2
Cholesterol (mg): 0
Carbohydrates (g): 40
Sodium (mg): 10
Dietary Fiber (g): 10.3

MEXICAN-STYLE CORN

When I was growing up, Mexican-style corn always meant corn kernels mixed with bits of red pepper. Here's a slightly rejiggered version that takes advantage of grilled fresh sweet peppers (both red and green), oniony chives and hot-buttered grilled corn on the cob. It was an instant winner with my family; I'm convinced it will be with yours.

PREPARATION TIME:
10 minutes

COOKING TIME:
15 minutes

SERVINGS: *4*

4	ears of corn, husked
	Butter-flavored cooking spray
1/2	teaspoon freshly ground black pepper
1/2	red sweet pepper
1/2	green sweet pepper
2	teaspoons whipped butter
1	teaspoon chopped chives

Preheat the grill. Coat a grill rack with cooking spray; place on the grill.

Spray the corn with the cooking spray and sprinkle the black pepper over each ear; wrap tightly with foil. Arrange on the grill rack; cook until tender, about 15 minutes. Arrange the sweet peppers on the rack; cook until tender, about 4 minutes on the first side, 3 minutes on the second.

Transfer the corn and peppers to a work surface. Cut the kernels from the corn and dice the peppers. Combine the peppers, corn, butter and chives in a bowl; toss to mix well.

HELPFUL HINT

Here's an easy way to cut corn kernels from the cob: Using a pot holder or tongs, hold the cob so it's standing on the wide end. Cut with a sharp knife from top to bottom.

PER SERVING:
Calories: 82
Fat (g): 2.1
Saturated Fat (g): 1
Cholesterol (mg): 4
Carbohydrates (g): 16.4
Sodium (mg): 19
Dietary Fiber (g): 2.2

MUSHROOM CAPS WITH GORGONZOLA CHEESE

Wow guests, family, anyone who's lucky enough to bite into one of these humble mushrooms. They're filled with fresh parsley and Gorgonzola cheese, Italy's famed blue cheese. Portobello mushrooms, which are large, meaty and firm are ideal for stuffing.

PREPARATION TIME:
5 to 10 minutes
COOKING TIME:
10 minutes
SERVINGS: **4**

1/2	cup soft bread crumbs
1/4	cup crumbled Gorgonzola cheese
1/2	teaspoon hot-pepper sauce
1/4	cup minced fresh parsley
4	large portobello mushrooms, stems removed

Preheat the grill and place a grill rack on the grill. Coat a grill basket or topper with cooking spray.

Combine the bread crumbs, cheese, pepper sauce and parsley in a small bowl. Spoon stuffing into the mushroom caps. Arrange, top of cap side down, on the grill basket or topper. Grill until hot throughout and the cheese filling is lightly browned, about 8 minutes. Serve immediately.

HELPFUL HINTS

Select large, meaty mushrooms with no signs of bruising or wilting.

Clean mushrooms by wiping them gently with a damp paper towel. Then carefully snap off the stems; they'll separate from the caps where the two join.

PER SERVING:
Calories: 50
Fat (g): 2.8
Saturated Fat (g): 1.7
Cholesterol (mg): 6.4
Carbohydrates (g): 3.9
Sodium (mg): 152
Dietary Fiber (g): 0.4

PARSLEY POTATOES

Refurbish an old favorite: parsley potatoes. It's easy to do. Give the stalwart potato fresh roasted flavor (instead of the usual boiled rendition), then let the hot potato soak up a simple butter topping. Finish with fresh parsley and black pepper. Simply superb.

PREPARATION TIME:
15 minutes

COOKING TIME:
30 minutes

SERVINGS: *4*

4   large potatoes
$^1/_4$ cup fat-free chicken broth
$^1/_2$ teaspoon whipped butter, melted
1   teaspoon olive oil
2   tablespoons minced fresh parsley
$^1/_2$ teaspoon freshly ground black pepper

Soak 4 bamboo skewers in water for 20 to 30 minutes. Preheat the grill. Coat a grill rack with cooking spray; place on the grill.

Microwave the potatoes on High until partially cooked, about 10 minutes. Transfer to a cutting board and quarter. Thread onto the skewers. Whisk with a wire whisk or a fork, the broth, butter and oil in a small bowl until well blended. Brush lightly over the potatoes.

Arrange on the grill rack. Grill over direct medium heat until the potatoes are tender, about 20 minutes, brushing with the broth mixture and turning frequently. Sprinkle the parsley and pepper over the potatoes.

HELPFUL HINTS

Four small new potatoes can replace 1 large potato.

Partially cooking the potatoes before grilling ensures quick, even cooking.

PER SERVING:
Calories: 163
Fat (g): 1.7
Saturated Fat (g): 0.4
Cholesterol (mg): 1
Carbohydrates (g): 34
Sodium (mg): 24
Dietary Fiber (g): 3.2

ROASTED POTATO SALAD

In this clever version of classic potato salad, grilled potatoes replace the standard boiled variety and sop up a zesty Dijon mustard and black pepper dressing. And onions and bacon are grilled to a golden-brown. Served warm or chilled, this recipe will surely charm its way into your collection.

10 to 12	small red or new potatoes (about 1 pound)
2	slices ($\frac{1}{2}$ ounce each) ready-to-eat Canadian bacon
12	white pearl onions
1	rib celery, chopped
2	cloves garlic, minced
2	teaspoons olive oil
2	teaspoons Dijon mustard
$\frac{1}{4}$	cup cider vinegar
$\frac{1}{4}$	cup plain nonfat yogurt
$\frac{1}{2}$	teaspoon freshly ground black pepper

PREPARATION TIME:
20 minutes
COOKING TIME:
25 minutes
SERVINGS: **4**

Preheat the grill and place a grill rack on the grill. Coat a grill basket or topper with cooking spray. Microwave the potatoes on High for 3 minutes.

Arrange the Canadian bacon, onions and potatoes in the grill basket. Grill over direct medium heat as follows: Grill the bacon just until lightly browned, about 5 minutes, turning with tongs or a spatula once; transfer to a platter and finely chop. Grill the onions until lightly browned and tender, about 7 minutes, turning with tongs or a spatula occasionally; transfer to a large bowl. Grill the potatoes until lightly browned and tender, about 20 minutes, turning with tongs occasionally; transfer to a platter and cut into bite-size pieces.

Add the bacon, potatoes, celery and garlic to the onions; toss gently to combine. Whisk the olive oil, mustard, vinegar, yogurt and pepper in a small bowl. Pour over the potato mixture; toss very gently to coat. Season with the pepper.

HELPFUL HINT

For best flavor, pour the mustard-pepper dressing over the potatoes while they're warm; cold potatoes won't absorb the flavors as readily.

PER SERVING:
Calories: 151
Fat (g): 3.3
Saturated Fat (g): 0.6
Cholesterol (mg): 4.4
Carbohydrates (g): 26.2
Sodium (mg): 152
Dietary Fiber (g): 2.5

SAUSAGE-STUFFED SWEET POTATOES WITH PEANUTS

Create a sensation in a shell—a sweet potato shell, that is. Mashed sweet potato with peanuts, grilled sausage and onions makes for a substantial main dish. Serve with crisp crackers and a beverage to complete the meal.

PREPARATION TIME:

20 minutes

COOKING TIME:

30 minutes

SERVINGS: **4**

2   large red sweet potatoes (about 2$\frac{1}{2}$ pounds)
2   small links maple-flavored sausage
$\frac{1}{2}$ onion, thinly sliced
1   cup fat-free, low-sodium beef broth
2   tablespoons chopped peanuts
1   jalapeño, seeded and chopped
$\frac{1}{4}$ cup chopped fresh cilantro
       Watercress leaves (garnish)

Preheat the grill and place a grill rack on the grill. Coat a grill basket or topper with cooking spray. Microwave the potatoes on High until tender, 12 to 18 minutes.

Arrange the sausage and onion in the basket or topper. Grill over direct medium heat until golden brown, 5 to 10 minutes, turning with tongs once or twice. Transfer to a work surface and coarsely chop.

Cut the potatoes in half lengthwise, and scoop out the flesh, transferring it to a large bowl and leaving $\frac{1}{4}$-inch shells intact. Stir the beef broth, peanuts, jalapeño, onion, sausage and cilantro into the flesh; mix thoroughly. Spoon into the shells, packing down as necessary. Wrap each shell in foil. Arrange on the grill. Grill until hot throughout, about 10 minutes. Garnish with the watercress and serve immediately.

HELPFUL HINT

Supermarkets often mislabel large, vitamin-A-rich, moist red sweet potatoes as yams. True yams are most often sold in Hispanic markets and have a white or pale yellow flesh.

PER SERVING:
Calories: 328
Fat (g): 11.3
Saturated Fat (g): 2.5
Cholesterol (mg): 10
Carbohydrates (g): 52.1
Sodium (mg): 319
Dietary Fiber (g): 5.3

SPINACH-STUFFED BUTTERNUT SQUASH

Stuffed squash makes a winning entrée—especially when it's grilled and perked up with spinach, cheddar cheese, and black olives, as this one is. Celery adds a surprising crunch in each bite. Serve as a satisfying vegetarian main dish or halve the recipe for a low-fuss side dish.

PREPARATION TIME:
15 minutes
COOKING TIME:
40 minutes
SERVINGS: *4*

2	medium butternut squash (about 3 pounds)
	Butter-flavored cooking spray
1/2	cup skim milk
1	rib celery, thinly sliced
1	cup torn baby spinach
1/2	cup shredded cheddar cheese
8	black olives, thinly sliced
1/2	teaspoon nutmeg
1/2	teaspoon freshly ground black pepper

Preheat the grill. Coat a grill rack with cooking spray; place on the grill. Cut the butternut squashes in half lengthwise; scoop out and discard the seeds. Mist both sides with the cooking spray. Arrange on the grill rack. Grill over direct low heat for 12 minutes. Turn with tongs or a spatula and grill for 20 minutes.

Transfer to a work surface. Scoop out the flesh, placing it in a large bowl and leaving the shells intact. Mash the flesh with a potato masher, adding the milk. Stir in the celery, spinach, cheddar cheese, olives, nutmeg and pepper. Spoon into the shells. Wrap in foil, and, keeping the shell side down, arrange on the grill. Heat until hot throughout, 5 to 10 minutes. Serve hot.

PER SERVING:
Calories: 199
Fat (g): 3.7
Saturated Fat (g): 1.8
Cholesterol (mg): 6
Carbohydrates (g): 39.1
Sodium (mg): 226
Dietary Fiber (g): 12.4

STUFFED EGGPLANT

Go Greek-style. This contemporary eggplant entrée gets its delightful accent from tomato, cinnamon, nutmeg, lemon and garlic. The dish, which comes together in minutes and is popular throughout Greece, makes for a light but satisfying main course. For heartier portions, increase the sirloin to ³/₄ pound and use medium-size eggplants.

PREPARATION TIME:

20 minutes

COOKING TIME:

25 minutes

SERVINGS: **4**

2	small eggplants (about 8 ounces each)
1	teaspoon olive oil
¹/₂	pound ground sirloin
1	small onion, chopped
4	cloves garlic, minced
¹/₂	cup herb-seasoned bread stuffing
1	tablespoon tomato paste
¹/₂	teaspoon cinnamon
¹/₂	teaspoon nutmeg
¹/₂	teaspoon grated lemon peel
¹/₂	cup nonfat sour cream

PER SERVING:
Calories: 210
Fat (g): 4.8
Saturated Fat (g): 1.5
Cholesterol (mg): 41
Carbohydrates (g): 20
Sodium (mg): 147
Dietary Fiber (g): 3.7

Preheat the grill. Coat a grill rack with cooking spray; place on the grill.

Cut the eggplants in half lengthwise, and, with a spoon, scoop out the centers, leaving ¹/₂-inch shells. Chop the pulp. Warm the olive oil in a medium-size nonstick skillet; add the sirloin, onion and garlic. Sauté until the sirloin is browned and crumbly, about 5 minutes, stirring occasionally. Add the eggplant pulp and sauté for 3 minutes, stirring constantly. Stir in the bread stuffing, tomato paste, cinnamon, nutmeg and lemon peel; mix well. Spoon into the eggplant shells. Wrap tightly in foil and arrange on the grill rack.

Grill over direct medium heat until hot throughout, about 15 minutes. Serve topped with the sour cream.

HELPFUL HINT

Use hot mitts for handling these food packets.

TOMATOES AND PEPPERS WITH PARMESAN VINAIGRETTE

Who can resist garden-fresh tomatoes? Or garden-fresh sweet peppers? I certainly can't—especially when they're dressed with fresh licorice-like basil and sharp-tasting Parmesan cheese. I think you'll find this is an uncomplicated dish with pleasingly complex flavors.

PREPARATION TIME:
10 minutes
COOKING TIME:
10 minutes
SERVINGS: **4**

1	teaspoon olive oil
2	teaspoons sugar
1/4	cup red wine vinegar
1	tablespoon grated Parmesan cheese
1/2	teaspoon freshly ground black pepper
1	teaspoon minced fresh basil
8	plum tomatoes
2	green sweet peppers, quartered

Whisk the oil, sugar, red wine vinegar, Parmesan cheese, black pepper and basil in a small bowl until well combined.

Preheat the grill. Coat a grill rack with cooking spray; place on the grill. Arrange the tomatoes and the sweet pepper quarters on the rack. Grill over indirect medium heat just until hot and very lightly browned, about 10 minutes, turning once with tongs.

Transfer to a serving platter and drizzle the Parmesan mixture over peppers and tomatoes.

HELPFUL HINTS

Avoid overcooking or charring the vegetables; too well done means an off-flavor.

Select tomatoes with no splits in their skins, and take care not to break the skins when turning the hot tomatoes.

Remove the seeds and membranes from the sweet peppers before cooking them.

PER SERVING:
Calories: 78
Fat (g): 4.2
Saturated Fat (g): 0.8
Cholesterol (mg): 1
Carbohydrates (g): 1
Sodium (mg): 34
Dietary Fiber (g): 2

TOMATOES STUFFED WITH DITALINI AND FONTINA

PREPARATION TIME:
15 minutes
COOKING TIME:
25 minutes
SERVINGS: *4*

This fuss-free recipe turns ordinary macaroni and cheese into a gourmet experience. Italian fontina cheese adds mild nutty taste. Hot-pepper sauce provides zing. Large, red ripe tomatoes encase each creamy serving. It's a dinnertime treat the entire family will love. But it's also special enough for company.

4	ounces ditalini
4	large tomatoes (about 12 ounces each)
4	ounces fontina cheese, shredded (1 cup)
$\frac{1}{2}$	red sweet pepper, chopped
2	teaspoons hot-pepper sauce
$\frac{1}{4}$	teaspoon paprika

Fill a large pot with water and bring to a boil. Add the ditalini and cook according to package directions until al dente; drain.

Preheat the grill. Coat a grill rack with cooking spray; place on the grill.

Cut the tops off the tomatoes and gently squeeze out the seeds. Discard the tops and seeds. Using a spoon, scoop out the pulp, leaving a thick wall. Coarsely chop the pulp. Combine the ditalini, fontina cheese, sweet pepper, $\frac{1}{4}$ cup tomato pulp, and the hot-pepper sauce in a medium-size bowl; stir to mix well. Spoon into the tomato shells. Sprinkle the paprika over the ditalini-cheese mixture.

Arrange on the grill rack. Grill, with the lid down, over medium direct heat until hot throughout and the cheese has melted, 7 to 12 minutes.

HELPFUL HINT

This recipe uses a mild hot-pepper sauce such as Crystal's. If you choose to substitute a hotter sauce such as Tabasco sauce, add it by drops, not teaspoonfuls, to achieve the hotness you desire.

PER SERVING:
Calories: 294
Fat (g): 10.5
Saturated Fat (g): 5.7
Cholesterol (mg): 33
Carbohydrates (g): 39
Sodium (mg): 271
Dietary Fiber (g): 4.7

ZUCCHINI WITH BASIL AND GARLIC

The ubiquitous and versatile zucchini—one of summer's treasures—gets a new look: For most dishes, this mild squash is julienned or cut into thin rounds. Not here. In this Italian-inspired recipe, it's sliced into long wide, thin strips, providing ample surface for brushing on a savory basil-balsamic baste. Each hot strip gets a quick dusting of sharp Parmesan cheese.

PREPARATION TIME:

10 minutes

COOKING TIME:

15 to 20 minutes

SERVINGS: *4*

2   teaspoons olive oil

1   tablespoon balsamic vinegar

2   cloves garlic, minced

5   basil leaves, finely chopped

1   medium zucchini, thinly sliced lengthwise (about 1 pound)

1   tablespoon grated Parmesan cheese

Preheat the grill and place a grill rack on the grill. Coat a grill basket or topper with cooking spray. Whisk the oil, balsamic vinegar, garlic and basil in a small bowl until well combined.

Arrange the zucchini on the grill basket. Grill over direct medium heat for 6 minutes. Turn with tongs or a spatula; brush the basil-balsamic mixture over the strips. Grill until tender, 8 to 10 minutes.

Using tongs or a spatula, transfer to a serving platter. Sprinkle the Parmesan cheese over each slice. Serve immediately.

HELPFUL HINT

A grill basket or topper isn't absolutely necessary for cooking the zucchini, but you do run the risk of the strips falling through the cracks.

PER SERVING:
Calories: 53
Fat (g): 2.7
Saturated Fat (g): 0.6
Cholesterol (mg): 1
Carbohydrates (g): 6.5
Sodium (mg): 28
Dietary Fiber (g): 1.4

positively poultry

Basil Chicken with Parmesan

Chicken Thighs Stuffed with Artichoke Hearts

Chicken with Hawaiian Pineapple Glaze

Five-Spice Drumsticks

Lemon Chicken with Roasted Red Pepper Sauce

Pepper Chicken with Grilled Garlic

Sesame Ginger Chicken Breasts

Szechuan Chicken Nuggets with Duck Sauce

Guava-Glazed Turkey Slices

Pepper Ham and Turkey Roll-ups

Turkey with Colby-Cream Sauce

Turkey with Fresh Plum Sauce

BASIL CHICKEN WITH PARMESAN

When you crave the special flavors of tomato, basil and cheese but want something fast from the grill, give this home-style parmigiana dish a shot. It's quick. It's easy. It's casual and satisfying.

PREPARATION TIME:

10 minutes

COOKING TIME:

20 minutes

SERVINGS: **4**

2	tablespoons ketchup
$\frac{1}{2}$	teaspoon olive oil
$\frac{1}{2}$	teaspoon freshly ground pepper
1	tablespoon minced fresh basil
$\frac{1}{4}$	teaspoon garlic powder
$\frac{3}{4}$	pound skinless, boneless chicken breast
2	tablespoons Parmesan cheese

Whisk the ketchup, oil, pepper, basil and garlic powder in a small bowl until well combined. Preheat the grill. Coat a grill rack with cooking spray; place on the grill. Arrange the chicken on the grill rack. Grill over indirect medium heat for 10 minutes. Turn with a spatula or tongs.

Spread the ketchup-basil mixture over the chicken. Grill until cooked through and the juices run clear, about 10 minutes. Transfer to a platter and sprinkle the Parmesan cheese over the chicken. Cut into serving-size pieces.

HELPFUL HINT

You could use dried basil (1 teaspoon) in this dish. Just be aware that it won't have the same sprightly taste.

PER SERVING:
Calories: 165
Fat (g): 4.4
Saturated Fat (g): 1.4
Cholesterol (mg): 74
Carbohydrates (g): 2.5
Sodium (mg): 198
Dietary Fiber (g): 0.2

CHICKEN THIGHS STUFFED WITH ARTICHOKE HEARTS

PREPARATION TIME:

10 minutes

COOKING TIME:

25 minutes

SERVINGS: *4*

Winningly delicious. Wonderfully simple. Recipes like this one—juicy chicken thighs stuffed with smoky gouda cheese and marinated artichoke hearts— give a whole new meaning to fast food. Ready to eat in 35 minutes or less.

4	skinless, boneless chicken thighs
4	marinated artichoke hearts
2	tablespoons gouda cheese
1	teaspoon olive oil
¼	cup seasoned bread crumbs

Preheat the grill and place a grill rack on the grill. Coat a grill basket or topper with cooking spray. Spread the chicken thighs on a work surface and place an artichoke heart and 1½ teaspoons gouda cheese in the center of each thigh. Roll up each thigh, encasing the artichoke and cheese in the center; secure with a metal skewer. Rub the oil over the outside of each roll. Coat with the bread crumbs.

Arrange on the grill basket. Grill over direct medium heat until cooked through and brown on all sides, 20 to 25 minutes, turning with tongs several times. Transfer to a platter; remove the skewers. Serve immediately.

HELPFUL HINT

The thighs can be secured with bamboo skewers; just be sure to soak them for 20 minutes before using them. Another fastening option is to tie thighs with kitchen string.

PER SERVING:
Calories: 184
Fat (g): 9.1
Saturated Fat (g): 3.2
Cholesterol (mg): 58
Carbohydrates (g): 7.1
Sodium (mg): 375
Dietary Fiber (g): 0.3

CHICKEN WITH HAWAIIAN PINEAPPLE GLAZE

Here's a pleasant, summery change of pace from standard barbecued chicken. The ultra-light pineapple glaze, which is no big deal to whip up, gets nice flavor and a hint of heat from hot-pepper sauce.

2	teaspoons olive oil
1/2	cup pineapple juice
1	teaspoon hot-pepper sauce
3/4	pound skinless, boneless chicken breasts
1 1/2	teaspoons cornstarch
4	slices pineapple

PREPARATION TIME:
10 minutes plus marinating
COOKING TIME:
25 minutes
SERVINGS: 4

Preheat the grill and place a grill rack on the grill. Coat a grill basket or topper with cooking spray. Whisk the olive oil, pineapple juice and hot-pepper sauce in a small bowl until well blended. Place the chicken and 1 tablespoon pineapple mixture into a self-sealing plastic bag, turning to coat well. Let marinate for 10 minutes.

Pour the remaining pineapple mixture into a small saucepan. Briskly whisk in the cornstarch. Cook over medium-high heat until thickened and clear, about 4 minutes, stirring constantly to prevent lumping.

Arrange the chicken on the grill basket or topper. Grill over direct medium heat for 10 minutes, turn with a spatula or tongs and brush with the pineapple mixture. Grill until lightly browned, cooked through and the juices run clear, about 10 minutes, brushing occasionally with the pineapple mixture.

Arrange the pineapple slices on the grill. Grill until lightly browned, about 10 minutes, turning once with a spatula. Serve chicken over pineapple slices.

HELPFUL HINT

For this recipe, you can use either fresh or canned pineapple slices. If using fresh, get canned unsweetened pineapple juice instead of trying to juice a pineapple yourself. If using canned pineapple slices, simply drain and reserve the juice for use in the recipe.

PER SERVING:
Calories: 190
Fat (g): 5.3
Saturated Fat (g): 1.2
Cholesterol (mg): 72
Carbohydrates (g): 7.6
Sodium (mg): 69
Dietary Fiber (g): 0.3

FIVE-SPICE DRUMSTICKS

To borrow from a well-known fast-food ad—these family-favorites are "finger-licking good." Happily, they're lean, too. So you can nibble on more than one, if you'd like. Each skinless drumstick is coated with a rich mixture of yogurt, five-spice powder and hoisin sauce (a sweet, spicy Chinese sauce made of soybeans, garlic, chili peppers and spices), then grilled. The sauce flavors up the chicken while keeping each piece exceedingly moist. This is a dinner winner, I think you'll agree.

PREPARATION TIME:
15 minutes plus
marinating
COOKING TIME:
35 to 45 minutes
SERVINGS: **6**

1	cup plain nonfat yogurt
1	small onion, minced
2	tablespoons hoisin sauce
1	tablespoon rice wine vinegar
$\frac{1}{2}$	teaspoon five-spice powder
6	chicken drumsticks (about 1$\frac{1}{2}$ pounds total)

Whisk the yogurt, onion, hoisin sauce, wine vinegar and five-spice powder in a small bowl until well blended. Skin the chicken. Place in a self-sealing plastic bag; add the yogurt-hoisin mixture, turning to coat well. Chill for 10 minutes, turning once.

Preheat the grill. Coat a grill rack with cooking spray; place on the grill. Remove the chicken from the bag, reserving the yogurt-hoisin mixture. Arrange on the grill rack. Grill over direct medium heat until the chicken is cooked through and the juices run clear, 35 to 45 minutes, turning occasionally and brushing with the yogurt-hoisin mixture once during the last 10 minutes of cooking. Discard any remaining yogurt-hoisin mixture.

HELPFUL HINT

To skin a drumstick: Hold it by the bone, grasp the skin with your other hand, and pull the skin up, inside out, and off the top.

PER SERVING:
Calories: 111
Fat (g): 2.7
Saturated Fat (g): 0.7
Cholesterol (mg): 42
Carbohydrates (g): 6.3
Sodium (mg): 142
Dietary Fiber (g): 0.3

LEMON CHICKEN WITH ROASTED RED PEPPER SAUCE

Testers raved: The lush roasted red sweet pepper sauce gives the lemony chicken plenty of personality as well as beautiful color. And adding the mild hot-pepper sauce to the lemon baste makes the whole dish sing without sting.

PREPARATION TIME:
20 minutes
COOKING TIME:
20 to 30 minutes
SERVINGS: **4**

- 2 teaspoons olive oil
- Juice of 1 lemon
- 3/4 teaspoon freshly ground black pepper
- 2 red sweet peppers
- 3/4 teaspoon hot-pepper sauce
- 1 pound skinless, boneless chicken breasts

Preheat the grill. Coat a grill rack with cooking spray; place on the grill. Whisk 1 teaspoon olive oil, the lemon juice and black pepper in a small bowl until well blended.

Arrange the peppers on the grill rack. Grill over direct medium heat until tender and slightly charred, 10 to 12 minutes, turning with tongs occasionally. Transfer to a glass baking dish with a lid or to a paper bag; close and let steam for 10 minutes. Rub off and discard the charred skin. Quarter the peppers and discard the seeds. Place in a food processor bowl; process at medium speed until pureed, stopping and scraping down the side of the bowl as necessary. Stir in the hot-pepper sauce.

Rub the remaining 1 teaspoon oil over the chicken. Arrange on the grill rack and grill over indirect medium heat until lightly browned and cooked through, 20 to 30 minutes, brushing frequently with the lemon mixture. Serve topped with the pureed peppers.

HELPFUL HINTS

The chicken is done when a meat thermometer registers 160°F and the juices run clear.

A food processor or a blender is needed to purée the roasted peppers.

PER SERVING:
Calories: 236
Fat (g): 6.5
Saturated Fat (g): 1.5
Cholesterol (mg): 96
Carbohydrates (g): 7.5
Sodium (mg): 90
Dietary Fiber (g): 1

PEPPER CHICKEN WITH GRILLED GARLIC

Use an entire head of garlic—on chicken? Why not? Garlic turns buttery, sweet and mild when roasted. But don't just take my word for it. Give it a try. You'll be an instant believer. In this recipe, roasted garlic and fresh rosemary make a sensational topping for simply grilled chicken breasts.

PREPARATION TIME:
10 minutes
COOKING TIME:
30 to 40 minutes
SERVINGS: *4*

1   whole head of garlic
2   teaspoons olive oil
2   teaspoons minced fresh rosemary
1   pound skinless, boneless chicken breast
1   teaspoon lemon pepper

Cut foil to create a 12-inch square. Remove the papery outer layers from the garlic. Cut off (and discard) the top of the garlic to expose the cloves. Place in the center of the foil. Drizzle 1 teaspoon oil over the top and sprinkle with the rosemary. Bring up the sides of the foil and twist the ends to seal.

Preheat the grill. Coat a grill rack with cooking spray; place on the grill. Place the garlic on the grill rack. Grill over direct medium heat until the cloves are soft, 30 to 40 minutes, turning with tongs once or twice.

Rub the remaining oil over the chicken and press in the lemon pepper. Arrange the chicken on the grill rack. Grill over direct medium heat until the chicken is cooked through and the juices run clear, 15 to 20 minutes, turning once with a spatula or tongs. Transfer the chicken to a serving plate. Open the foil and carefully squeeze the softened garlic over the chicken. Slice and serve.

HELPFUL HINT

The longer (within reason) the garlic roasts the better. So feel free to leave it on the grill for an hour, if you have the time.

PER SERVING:
Calories: 228
Fat (g): 6.4
Saturated Fat (g): 1.5
Cholesterol (mg): 96
Carbohydrates (g): 4.8
Sodium (mg): 166
Dietary Fiber (g): 0.3

SESAME GINGER CHICKEN BREASTS

Imagine tender chicken infused with enticing sweet-salty teriyaki and nutty sesame flavors. Is your mouth watering yet? I hope so, for those are the delightful flavors you'll find in this trendy entrée.

PREPARATION TIME:
10 minutes plus marinating
COOKING TIME:
20 minutes
SERVINGS: *4*

1	teaspoon sesame seeds
1	teaspoon sesame oil
2	tablespoons low-sodium soy sauce
1	tablespoon dry sherry
1	teaspoon sugar
1	tablespoon minced gingerroot
1/4	teaspoon cayenne
1	pound skinless, boneless chicken breasts

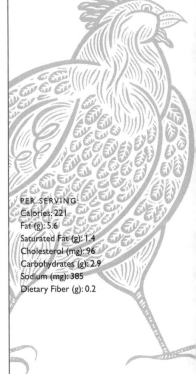

Whisk the sesame seeds, sesame oil, soy sauce, sherry, sugar, gingerroot and cayenne in a small bowl until well combined. Place the chicken in a self-sealing bag; pour in the sesame mixture, turning to coat well. Marinate in the refrigerator for 30 minutes; drain the sesame mixture into a small saucepan. Bring to a boil over medium-high heat; cook for 2 minutes.

Preheat the grill. Coat a grill rack with cooking spray; place on the grill. Arrange the chicken on the grill rack. Grill over indirect medium heat until done and the juices run clear, about 20 minutes, turning once with a spatula or tongs and brushing occasionally with the sesame mixture.

HELPFUL HINTS

If you're in a big hurry, cut the marinating time to 10 minutes. But if you can spare up to 4 hours for marinating, let the chicken soak up maximum flavor. Boiling the marinade helps blend and concentrate the flavors.

Remember to heat any sauce that's been in contact with raw or partially cooked meat or poultry before serving it.

PER SERVING:
Calories: 221
Fat (g): 5.6
Saturated Fat (g): 1.4
Cholesterol (mg): 96
Carbohydrates (g): 2.9
Sodium (mg): 385
Dietary Fiber (g): 0.2

SZECHUAN CHICKEN NUGGETS WITH DUCK SAUCE

PREPARATION TIME:

10 minutes

COOKING TIME:

15 minutes

SERVINGS: *4*

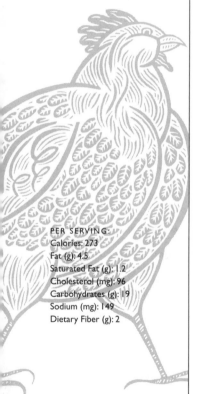

PER SERVING:
Calories: 273
Fat (g): 4.5
Saturated Fat (g): 1.2
Cholesterol (mg): 96
Carbohydrates (g): 19
Sodium (mg): 149
Dietary Fiber (g): 2

Create a sensational dish with just four ingredients. That's right, just four: chicken nuggets that are coated with duck sauce, then dusted with whole wheat flour and Szechuan seasoning. The chicken is tender and juicy; the crust, rustic with a subtle sweet-savory flavor. Family and friends will request these crunchy bite-size morsels often.

$\frac{1}{2}$ cup whole wheat flour

1 tablespoon Szechuan seasoning

1 pound skinless, boneless chicken breast, cut into 1-inch cubes

$\frac{1}{4}$ cup duck sauce

Preheat the grill and place a grill rack on the grill. Coat a grill basket or topper with cooking spray. Whisk the flour and Szechuan seasoning in a small bowl until well combined.

Place the chicken in a self-sealing plastic bag; add the duck sauce, turning to coat well. Remove from the bag and dredge in the flour mixture. Arrange in the basket or topper. Grill until lightly browned on all sides and cooked through, about 15 minutes, turning with tongs occasionally. Serve immediately with additional duck sauce for dipping if desired.

HELPFUL HINTS

Duck sauce and Szechuan seasoning are available in almost any well-stocked supermarket.

The chicken can be marinated in the duck sauce for up to 8 hours if you wish.

GUAVA-GLAZED TURKEY SLICES

Hailing from warm climes, fragrant guava makes a marvelously agreeable brush-on for turkey (or chicken if you wish). Here, a small amount of the cornstarch thickens the warmed guava jelly so it clings very nicely. And a dash of thyme-like savory provides an interesting kick.

PREPARATION TIME:

10 minutes

COOKING TIME:

30 minutes

SERVINGS: **4**

1/2 cup guava jelly

1 teaspoon cornstarch

1/8 teaspoon dried savory

2 teaspoons whipped butter, melted

1 pound skinless, boneless turkey breast slices

Combine the guava jelly, cornstarch and savory in a small saucepan over medium-low heat, stirring to mix well. Simmer the mixture for 2 minutes, stirring constantly.

Preheat the grill. Coat a grill rack with cooking spray; place on the grill. Brush the butter over both sides of the turkey slices. Arrange on the grill rack. Grill over indirect medium heat for 15 minutes and turn with a spatula or tongs. Brush with the guava glaze. Cook until the turkey is cooked through, 8 to 12 minutes, brushing occasionally with the glaze.

HELPFUL HINTS

If turkey breast slices are unavailable, get turkey cutlets. Adjust cooking time as necessary for the thickness of the cutlets.

Don't boil the guava mixture vigorously or after it has thickened; heated too much, cornstarch breaks down and thins.

PER SERVING:
Calories: 272
Fat (g): 2.4
Saturated Fat (g): 1.2
Cholesterol (mg): 98
Carbohydrates (g): 28
Sodium (mg): 73
Dietary Fiber (g): 0.4

PEPPER HAM AND TURKEY ROLL-UPS

Turkey goes haute cuisine. This is the way it's done: Thin slices are wrapped jelly-roll fashion with pepper ham, Jarlsberg cheese and roasted red peppers, then dressed with Zinfandel. This entrée may sound complex, but it's really quite easy to prepare and is ready to serve in just 40 minutes. If you wish, another dry white wine can be substituted for the Zinfandel.

PREPARATION TIME:
10 minutes
COOKING TIME:
30 minutes
SERVINGS: *4*

$^1/_2$ cup white Zinfandel
2   teaspoons olive oil
2   tablespoons minced fresh thyme
4   skinless, boneless turkey breast slices (about 1 pound)
4   thin slices ($^1/_2$ ounce each) deli pepper ham
2   ounces Jarlsberg cheese, shredded
$^1/_2$ cup roasted red peppers, chopped

Soak 4 bamboo skewers in water to cover in a shallow baking dish for 30 minutes. Whisk the Zinfandel, oil and thyme in a small bowl until well combined. Preheat the grill. Coat a grill rack with cooking spray; place on the grill.

Place the turkey in a sturdy plastic bag; pound with a meat mallet to $^1/_8$ inch thick. Layer the turkey, ham, Jarlsberg cheese and red peppers, starting with the turkey and dividing the ingredients evenly. Roll up jelly-roll style and fasten with a bamboo skewer. Secure with kitchen string.

Arrange on the grill rack. Grill over direct medium heat for 7 minutes. Brush on the Zinfandel mixture. Turn. Grill until cooked through, tender and no longer pink, 20 to 25 minutes, turning twice and brushing twice with the Zinfandel mixture.

HELPFUL HINT

Keep the cheese and peppers near the center of the turkey roll or they'll fall into the grill during cooking.

PER SERVING:
Calories: 265
Fat (g): 7.2
Saturated Fat (g): 2.7
Cholesterol (mg): 109
Carbohydrates (g): 2.7
Sodium (mg): 252
Dietary Fiber (g): 0.5

70

TURKEY WITH COLBY-CREAM SAUCE

Few recipes can boast such a luxurious sauce—sour cream, colby cheese and Madeira. Here, it enhances perfectly grilled turkey breast slices, but you could use it on chicken or pork with equally delicious results. I think you'll find it very agreeable and a dish you prepare often.

PREPARATION TIME:

20 minutes

COOKING TIME:

15 minutes

SERVINGS: **4**

- 1/2 cup nonfat sour cream
- 2 ounces colby cheese, shredded
- 2 tablespoons Madeira
- 1 shallot, minced
- 1/4 teaspoon freshly ground black pepper
- 1 pound turkey breast slices

Preheat the grill and place a grill rack on the grill. Coat a grill basket or topper with cooking spray. Whisk the sour cream, colby cheese, Madeira, shallot and pepper in a small saucepan until well combined. Heat over medium-low heat just until the cheese melts, stirring gently and constantly. Divide the mixture in half, reserving 1 portion for serving with the cooked turkey.

Arrange the turkey on the basket or topper. Grill over direct medium heat for 5 minutes. Turn with tongs or a spatula and brush with the colby sauce. Grill until tender and no longer pink, about 10 minutes, brushing with the colby mixture several times. Discard the sauce used for basting. Serve with the reserved sauce.

HELPFUL HINT

A lean meat, turkey breast is easily overcooked. Remove it from the heat when just done, but not before.

PER SERVING:
Calories: 272
Fat (g): 5.4
Saturated Fat (g): 3.1
Cholesterol (mg): 108
Carbohydrates (g): 9.8
Sodium (mg): 182
Dietary Fiber (g): 0

TURKEY WITH FRESH PLUM SAUCE

Use any variety of ripe plum in this sweet and fruity sauce, which tastes similar to homemade applesauce. Love one and you'll surely love the other. Remember, the color, texture and flavor of the sauce will vary with the plum variety. If the plum size is quite small, use three instead of two. The hot-pepper sauce should be a mild one such as Crystal's.

PREPARATION TIME:
15 minutes

COOKING TIME:
15 minutes

SERVINGS: *4*

2 plums, peeled and pitted
2 tablespoons raspberry vinegar
1 teaspoon light brown sugar
$1/4$ teaspoon hot-pepper sauce
2 teaspoons olive oil
1 pound turkey breast cutlets
$1/2$ teaspoon freshly ground black pepper
2 tablespoons minced fresh sage

For the plum sauce, combine the plums, raspberry vinegar, brown sugar and hot-pepper sauce in the bowl of a mini-food processor; process until pureed. Transfer to a small stainless steel, nonstick or enamel saucepan. Simmer over medium heat, stirring constantly until slightly reduced, about 7 minutes. Keep warm.

Preheat the grill. Coat a grill rack with cooking spray; place on the grill. Rub the oil over the turkey cutlets. Arrange on the grill rack. Grill over indirect medium heat for 5 to 10 minutes, depending on thickness. Turn, using a spatula or tongs. Season with the pepper and sage. Grill until cooked through and juices run clear, 5 to 10 minutes depending on thickness. Serve topped with the plum sauce.

HELPFUL HINTS

Oiling the cutlets will help them brown without drying out.

The plum sauce can be served warm or chilled.

PER SERVING:
Calories: 199
Fat (g): 3.4
Saturated Fat (g): 0.6
Cholesterol (mg): 94
Carbohydrates (g): 6.2
Sodium (mg): 61
Dietary Fiber (g): 0.6

easy dinner platters

Asian Pork with Peanut Sauce

Beef and Avocado Stir-Fry

Caribbean Cod Platter

Chicken Pineapple Salad with Mafalda

Chicken Provençal Brochettes

Pork with Peanut Noodles

Sesame Pork Tenderloin Platter

Spaghetti with Hot Italian Sausage Sauce

Spicy Chicken and Vegetables Stir-Fry

Veal Chops Marsala with Peppers and Belgian Endive

Warm Sea Scallop Salad with Mesclun

Lobster Bake

ASIAN PORK WITH PEANUT SAUCE

Earn dinnertime praise with this winningly simple meal. A sprightly peanut sauce imparts heady flavors and aromas to juicy pork chops and a jumble of nutty-tasting Chinese wheat noodles. Lightly cooked green peas add sparkling color and freshness. You'll find the meal substantial enough for the heartiest of appetites and graceful enough for company.

PREPARATION TIME:

20 minutes plus marinating

COOKING TIME:

30 minutes

SERVINGS: **4**

3	tablespoons peanut sauce
3	tablespoons lemon juice
¾	pound center-cut pork loin chops
1½	cups peas
8	ounces Chinese wheat noodles
¾	cup beef broth
1	tablespoon cornstarch

Whisk the peanut sauce and lemon juice in a small bowl. Place the pork chops and 2 tablespoons of the peanut sauce mixture in a self-sealing plastic bag, turning to coat well. Let marinate in the refrigerator for 30 minutes to 8 hours.

Preheat the grill. Coat a grill rack with cooking spray; place on the grill. Arrange the pork on the grill rack. Grill over indirect medium heat until the chops are cooked through, about 20 minutes, turning once with a spatula or tongs and brushing once with the peanut sauce mixture. Transfer to a platter and cut into thin strips. Cover with foil to keep warm.

Fill a large pot with water and bring to a boil over high heat. Add the peas and Chinese noodles. Cook, uncovered, over medium heat for 3 minutes; drain.

Whisk the beef broth, cornstarch and remaining peanut sauce mixture in a saucepan until the cornstarch is dissolved and the mixture well blended. Cook over medium heat until thickened slightly, stirring constantly. Stir in the pork. Divide the noodles among 4 dinner plates. Top with the pork and peanut sauce.

PER SERVING:
Calories: 465
Fat (g): 9.5
Saturated Fat (g): 2.7
Cholesterol (mg): 70
Carbohydrates (g): 57
Sodium (mg): 347
Dietary Fiber (g): 6.8

HELPFUL HINT

Start marinating the pork early in the day if possible. Longer marinating imparts more flavor than a quick soak.

BEEF AND AVOCADO STIR-FRY

Stir-frying—on the grill? You bet your wok! The intense heat is perfect for fast cooking. And the technique imparts oh-so-good smoky flavors. Use one of the new-fangled grill woks with all those little holes to let in the smoke yet prevent food from falling into the grill. This stir-fry is Mexican-inspired with zesty picante sauce, nippy lime juice, red peppers and cumin—all topped with soothing sour cream.

PREPARATION TIME:

20 minutes plus marinating

COOKING TIME:

20 minutes

SERVINGS: *4*

1	cup mild picante sauce
	Juice of 1 lime
¾	pound sirloin beef steak, cut into very thin short strips
1	cup wild pecan rice
½	teaspoon ground cumin
1	red sweet pepper, cut into bite-size pieces
1	small onion, cut into thin wedges
4	medium yellow tomatoes, seeded and cut into bite-size pieces
1	Florida avocado, cut into bite-size pieces
1	cup fat-free sour cream

Whisk the picante sauce and lime juice in a small bowl. Place the beef strips and ¼ cup of the picante mixture in a self-sealing plastic bag, turning to coat all pieces. Let marinate in the refrigerator for 30 minutes to 8 hours; drain.

Cook the rice according to package directions, adding the cumin and omitting the butter and salt. Transfer to a large serving bowl and cover with foil to keep warm.

Preheat the grill and place a grill rack on the grill. Coat a grill wok with cooking spray and place on the grill rack. Spoon in the beef. Stir-fry over medium direct heat until lightly browned and almost cooked through, about 5 minutes, using a long-handled spoon or spatula to flip and turn the beef often. Add the sweet pepper and mix well. Stir-fry for 4 minutes. Add the onion and mix well. Stir-fry for 3 minutes. Add the tomatoes and mix well. Stir-fry for 1 minute.

Warm the remaining picante mixture in a small saucepan over medium heat on the stove top or in a microwave-safe bowl in the microwave at Medium. Spoon the beef-vegetable mixture over the rice and drizzle the picante mixture over the top. Serve with the avocado and sour cream.

HELPFUL HINTS

Avocado pieces darken, or oxidize, quickly. To slow the process, dip cut avocado in lemon or lime juice.

To seed tomatoes, cut them in half crosswise. Gently squeeze to force out the seeds and excess juice.

PER SERVING:
Calories: 140
Fat (g): 3.5
Saturated Fat (g): 0.9
Cholesterol (mg): 18
Carbohydrates (g): 17
Sodium (mg): 154
Dietary Fiber (g): 2.3

CARIBBEAN COD PLATTER

Sample exquisite island cuisine without leaving the comfort of your landlocked patio. Here, sofrito sauce infuses its spicy flavors into sweet potatoes and mild codfish while Spanish capers add a salty, pungent surprise to each bite. Though not native to the Caribbean, codfish is readily available in most supermarkets and adapts splendidly to grilling as well as Caribbean flavors. Spanish capers are larger than their nonpareil cousins, but have the same distinctive taste.

PREPARATION TIME:

10 minutes

COOKING TIME:

20 minutes

SERVINGS: *4*

1	pound codfish steaks
1	pound sweet potatoes, peeled and cut into $1/4$-inch slices
1	medium Spanish onion, cut into $1/4$-inch slices
2	bananas, peeled and quartered lengthwise
$1/4$	cup sofrito sauce
2	tablespoons Spanish capers
	Cilantro sprigs (garnish)

Preheat the grill and place a grill rack on the grill. Coat a grill basket or topper with cooking spray. Arrange the cod, potatoes, onion and bananas on the rack. Grill over direct medium heat until the cod flakes and the potatoes are tender, about 20 minutes, basting with the sofrito sauce and turning with a spatula or tongs once.

Serve the onion slices over the potatoes and the capers over the fish. Arrange the bananas on the side of the dish and garnish with the cilantro.

HELPFUL HINTS

To determine if cod (or any other fish) is done, probe the flesh gently with the tip of a sharp knife. It's ready to eat when the flesh flakes easily and appears opaque from top to bottom.

In this recipe, the bananas may be done before the rest of the food. If they are, transfer them to a serving platter and cover them with foil to keep them warm until everything else is tender and cooked through.

PER SERVING:

Calories: 351

Fat (g): 7.3

Saturated Fat (g): 1.9

Cholesterol (mg): 67

Carbohydrates (g): 43

Sodium (mg): 442

Dietary Fiber (g): 4.7

CHICKEN PINEAPPLE SALAD WITH MAFALDA

Wake up your palate with this refreshing, warm pasta salad. Fresh cilantro with its unique cuminlike essence graces the lively pineapple vinaigrette. Bright red cherry tomatoes play well with sweet pineapple chunks. And the whole meal is ready to eat in less than 45 minutes.

PREPARATION TIME:
15 to 20 minutes
COOKING TIME:
20 minutes
SERVINGS: *4*

8	ounces mafalda
2	teaspoons olive oil
$\frac{1}{2}$	cup pineapple juice
$\frac{1}{2}$	teaspoon crushed red pepper flakes
24	cherry tomatoes
1	cup pineapple chunks
$\frac{3}{4}$	pound skinless, boneless chicken breasts
2	tablespoons white wine vinegar
2	teaspoons powdered pectin
2	tablespoons minced fresh cilantro
1	scallion, minced

Fill a large pot with water and bring to a boil over high heat. Add the mafalda and reduce the heat to low. Cook, uncovered, according to package directions until al dente; drain.

Whisk the olive oil, pineapple juice and red pepper in a small bowl until well blended. Place the tomatoes, pineapple and 1 tablespoon pineapple juice mixture in a self-sealing plastic bag, turning to coat. Using a slotted spoon, remove the tomatoes and pineapple. Place the chicken and 1 tablespoon pineapple juice mixture in the bag, turning to coat.

Preheat the grill. Coat a grill rack with cooking spray; place on the grill. Coat a grill basket or topper with cooking spray. Arrange the tomatoes and pineapple chunks on the grill basket. Grill over medium direct heat until hot and lightly brown, about 5 minutes, turning occasionally with tongs. Carefully transfer to a large bowl.

Arrange the chicken on the grill rack. Grill over indirect medium heat until lightly browned, cooked through and the juices run clear, about 20 minutes, turning once with a spatula. Transfer to a platter and cut into thin, short strips. Add the tomatoes and pineapple. Add the mafalda; toss gently to combine.

Stir the white wine vinegar, pectin, cilantro and scallions into the remaining pineapple mixture. Mix until well combined. Pour over the chicken-pasta mixture; toss to coat.

HELPFUL HINTS

In this recipe, bow tie pasta can replace the mafalda, or tiny lasagna noodles.

There's no need to buy pineapple juice; simply drain canned pineapple chunks and reserve the juice.

Take care not to overcook the tomatoes. Remove them from the heat just before they split and lose their juices.

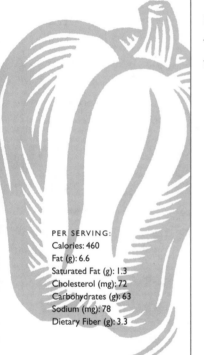

PER SERVING:
Calories: 460
Fat (g): 6.6
Saturated Fat (g): 1.3
Cholesterol (mg): 72
Carbohydrates (g): 63
Sodium (mg): 78
Dietary Fiber (g): 3.3

CHICKEN PROVENÇAL BROCHETTES

Brochettes are the French version of kabobs—tasty skewered and grilled-to-perfection meats and vegetables. Note the special treatment of zucchini. Here, this ubiquitous and always popular vegetable is cut into wide strips instead of the usual disk-shaped slices.

PREPARATION TIME:
20 to 30 minutes
COOKING TIME:
20 minutes
SERVINGS: **4**

  2 teaspoons olive oil
  2 teaspoons herbes de Provence
  I teaspoon freshly ground black pepper
  3/4 pound skinless, boneless chicken breasts, cut into 1-inch cubes
  8 ounces small white mushroom caps
  I small zucchini, quartered lengthwise and cut into 1/4-inch slices
  I yellow sweet pepper, cut into 1-inch pieces

Place 8 bamboo skewers in a shallow baking dish; cover with water. Let soak for 30 minutes.

Preheat the grill. Coat a grill rack with cooking spray; place on the grill. Whisk I teaspoon oil, I teaspoon herbs de Provence and 1/2 teaspoon pepper in a small bowl until well combined. Place the chicken in a self-sealing bag; spoon in the herbes de Provence mixture, turning to coat all pieces well. Thread onto skewers. Arrange on the grill rack. Grill over direct medium heat until lightly browned, cooked through and juices run clear, about 20 minutes, turning several times.

Whisk the remaining I teaspoon oil, I teaspoon herbes de Provence and 1/2 teaspoon pepper in a small bowl until well combined. Place the mushrooms, zucchini, sweet pepper and herbes de Provence mixture in a self-sealing bag, turning gently to coat well. Thread onto skewers. Arrange on the grill rack. Grill until lightly browned on all sides and tender, about 20 minutes, turning several times.

Thread meat and vegetables onto 2 skewers placed about $\frac{1}{4}$ inch apart so the food doesn't twist and turn during cooking.

Rosemary, marjoram, thyme, sage and savory make up the basic herbes de Provence blend, which is typical of southern France. If you can't find the mix, use any of the individual herbs. But stick with dried, which will hold up well during grilling.

HELPFUL HINTS

Place the herb mixture in the self-sealing bag last or it will stick to the bag, not to the food.

PER SERVING:
Calories: 201
Fat (g): 5.7
Saturated Fat (g): 1.2
Cholesterol (mg): 72
Carbohydrates (g): 7.8
Sodium (mg): 69
Dietary Fiber (g): 2

PORK WITH PEANUT NOODLES

Take a cue from Asian cuisines. And make judicious use of peanuts with their crunchy texture and melt-in-your-mouth flavor. Here, they're tossed with lean pork, crisp-tender florets of broccoli and translucent bean thread noodles, which have soaked up a pleasingly hot Asian-style sauce.

PREPARATION TIME:
25 minutes plus marinating
COOKING TIME:
25 minutes
SERVINGS: **4**

1	tablespoon low-sodium soy sauce
1	teaspoon peanut oil
2	teaspoons Chinese chili sauce with garlic
2	tablespoons rice wine vinegar
3/4	pound boneless center-cut loin pork chops
7 1/2	ounces bean thread noodles
2	cups small broccoli florets
4	scallions, minced
1/2	cup fat-free, low-sodium beef broth
2	tablespoons chopped peanuts

Whisk the soy sauce, peanut oil, Chinese chili sauce and rice vinegar in a small microwave-safe bowl. Place the pork chops in a self-sealing plastic bag. Spoon in 1 tablespoon of the soy sauce mixture, turning to coat well. Marinate in the refrigerator for at least 20 minutes. Soak bean threads in water for 10 minutes.

Preheat the grill. Coat a grill rack with cooking spray; place on the grill. Arrange the pork on the grill rack. Grill over indirect medium heat until done and the juices run clear, about 20 minutes, turning once with a spatula or tongs. Transfer to a platter and cut into bite-size pieces. Cover with foil to keep warm.

Fill a large pot with water and bring to a boil. Add the broccoli and cook for 2 minutes. Add the scallions and bean thread noodles. Cook for 2 minutes; drain thoroughly.

Whisk the beef broth into the remaining soy sauce mixture. Microwave at Medium-High just until hot, 30 to 60 seconds. Combine the noodle mixture, the pork, the peanuts and the soy sauce mixture in a large bowl, tossing to mix well. Serve immediately.

HELPFUL HINT

The pork chops can be marinated, in the refrigerator, for up to 24 hours. Store the reserved soy sauce mixture, covered, in the refrigerator.

PER SERVING:
Calories: 369
Fat (g): 8.9
Saturated Fat (g): 2.4
Cholesterol (mg): 46
Carbohydrates (g): 50
Sodium (mg): 256
Dietary Fiber (g): 2.2

SESAME PORK TENDERLOIN PLATTER

Take the heat off the kitchen. And cook tonight's dinner outside on the grill. With this recipe you'll feast on succulent pork tenderloin; juicy, slightly tart cherry tomatoes; tiny sweet pearl onions—all seasoned with a sensational sesame-teriyaki sauce.

PREPARATION TIME:
10 minutes plus marinating
COOKING TIME:
30 to 35 minutes
SERVINGS: *4*

²⁄₃	cup rice wine vinegar
2	tablespoons reduced-sodium soy sauce
1	teaspoon toasted sesame seeds
4	cloves garlic, crushed
1	tablespoon peanut oil
1	pork tenderloin (about 1 pound)
8	small red potatoes
24	cherry tomatoes
16	pearl onions
4	cups coarsely cut napa cabbage

For the marinade and dressing, whisk the vinegar, soy sauce, sesame seeds, garlic and oil in a small bowl until well blended. Divide the mixture in half; use half for the marinade and the remaining for the dressing.

Place the pork in a self-sealing plastic bag. Pour in the marinade, turning to coat well. Chill at least 20 minutes, turning once.

Preheat the grill and place a grill rack on the grill. Coat a grill basket or topper with cooking spray. Remove the pork from the bag, reserving the marinade. Arrange on the basket or topper. Grill over direct medium heat until the juice is clear (160°F on a meat thermometer), 30 to 35 minutes, brushing occasionally with the marinade up to the last 5 minutes of cooking. Discard any marinade left from grilling. Allow to sit for 5 minutes; slice thinly.

Cook the potatoes in the microwave for 5 minutes. Arrange on the grill basket near the pork. Grill until tender, about 20 minutes, brushing occasionally with the marinade up to the last 5 minutes of cooking and turning with tongs several times.

Arrange the tomatoes and onions on the grill topper. Grill until hot, about 5 minutes, turning with tongs once. Serve the pork atop the cabbage. Arrange the tomatoes, onions and potatoes next to the pork. Drizzle the reserved dressing over the pork and vegetables.

HELPFUL HINT

Marinating the pork for up to 8 hours will intensify the sesame-garlic flavor imparted by the marinade.

PER SERVING:
Calories: 374
Fat (g): 9.6
Saturated Fat (g): 2.6
Cholesterol (mg): 89
Carbohydrates (g): 31
Sodium (mg): 381
Dietary Fiber (g): 4.6

SPAGHETTI WITH HOT ITALIAN SAUSAGE SAUCE

A time-honored family favorite just got better as the pleasant smoky flavors of grilled onion, fennel and Italian sausage replace the usual sautéed versions. The tomato base is simple and fresh. My family loves the combination; I'm sure yours will, too.

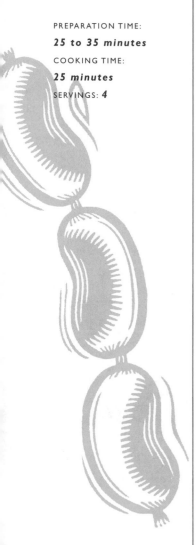

PREPARATION TIME:
25 to 35 minutes

COOKING TIME:
25 minutes

SERVINGS: **4**

1	can (28 ounces) plum tomatoes, cut up
$^1/_4$	cup minced fresh parsley
4	cloves garlic, crushed
8	basil leaves, minced
$^1/_4$	teaspoon ground celery seeds
$^1/_2$	teaspoon hot-pepper sauce
$^1/_2$	teaspoon sugar
1	small fennel bulb, trimmed and cut into very thin wedges
1	small onion, cut into thin wedges
$^1/_4$	pound hot Italian sausage
8	ounces spaghetti
	Grated Parmesan cheese (garnish)

Preheat the grill and place a grill rack on the grill. Coat a grill wok, basket or topper with cooking spray.

Combine the plum tomatoes, parsley, garlic, basil leaves, celery seeds, hot-pepper sauce and sugar in a 3-quart saucepan, stirring until well mixed. Simmer, covered, over medium heat for 10 minutes, stirring occasionally.

Arrange the fennel, onion and sausage in the wok. Grill over direct medium heat until the fennel and onion are lightly browned and tender and the sausage is cooked through and browned, about 25 minutes, stirring the vegetables and turning the sausage occasionally. (Remove the vegetables when they are done.) Add the fennel and onion to the tomato mixture; stir to mix well. Slice the sausage thinly and add to the tomato mixture; stir to mix well.

Fill a large pot with water and bring to a boil over high heat. Add the spaghetti and reduce the heat to medium. Cook, uncovered, according to package directions until al dente; drain. Serve topped with the tomato mixture. Garnish with the Parmesan cheese.

HELPFUL HINT

The onion and fennel may be done before the sausage. If so, transfer them to the tomato sauce and continue cooking the sausage until it's cooked through.

PER SERVING:
Calories: 372
Fat (g): 9
Saturated Fat (g): 2.8
Cholesterol (mg): 22
Carbohydrates (g): 58
Sodium (mg): 305
Dietary Fiber (g): 5.2

SPICY CHICKEN AND VEGETABLES STIR-FRY

There's nothing shy about this stir-fry. It has a spicy Asian-style kick from Szechuan sauce, which you can pick up in almost any supermarket. Look to the tiny broccoli florets, baby carrots and baby corn for a balance of vibrant vegetable textures and flavors and a riot of bright color.

PREPARATION TIME:
10 to 15 minutes

COOKING TIME:
25 to 30 minutes

SERVINGS: **4**

$^1/_2$ pound baby carrots

1$^3/_4$ cups broccoli florets

$^3/_4$ cup chicken broth

1 tablespoon cornstarch

2 teaspoons Szechuan sauce

$^3/_4$ pound skinless, boneless chicken breast tenders

1 can (8 ounces) baby corn, drained

1$^1/_2$ cups sliced bok choy

Place the carrots in a microwave-safe bowl; add 2 tablespoons water. Microwave, covered, on High for 2 minutes. Add the broccoli, cover, and microwave on High for 1 minute.

Whisk the chicken broth, cornstarch and Szechuan sauce in a small saucepan until well blended. Cook over medium heat until slightly thickened, about 3 minutes, stirring constantly. Keep warm.

Preheat the grill and place a grill rack on the grill. Coat a grill wok, basket or topper with cooking spray. Place the chicken in the wok. Stir-fry over direct medium heat until the chicken is almost cooked through and is starting to brown, about 10 minutes, stirring often. Add the baby corn and stir to mix. Stir-fry for 6 minutes. Add the bok choy, broccoli and carrots; stir to mix. Stir-fry until the vegetables are hot and tender, 2 to 5 minutes.

Transfer to a bowl and add the Szechuan mixture. Toss gently to coat.

HELPFUL HINT

Of all the vegetables in this dish, carrots take the most cooking. Test them for doneness. If they're tender all the others will be, too.

PER SERVING:
Calories: 240
Fat (g): 3.6
Saturated Fat (g): 1
Cholesterol (mg): 72
Carbohydrates (g): 22
Sodium (mg): 152
Dietary Fiber (g): 5.2

VEAL CHOPS MARSALA WITH PEPPERS AND BELGIAN ENDIVE

For sophisticated palates: Tender juicy veal coated with a slightly caramelized sweet Marsala sauce and accompanied by cheerful red pepper strips and young heads of Belgian endive. Worthy of company, this entrée is simple enough for weeknight dining.

PREPARATION TIME:
15 minutes
COOKING TIME:
25 minutes
SERVINGS: *4*

2	teaspoons butter
2	scallions, white part only, chopped
1/4	teaspoon lemon pepper
1/2	cup sweet Marsala
1/4	cup grated Parmesan cheese
1/4	cup finely chopped arugula leaves
1	pound thick veal loin chops
2	red sweet peppers, cut into thin strips
4	small heads Belgian endive

Preheat the grill. Coat a grill rack with cooking spray; place on the grill. Coat a grill basket or topper with cooking spray.

Melt the butter in a small skillet over medium-high heat. Add the scallions and lemon pepper; sauté until the scallions are golden, about 3 minutes. Remove from the heat and stir in the Marsala, Parmesan cheese and arugula leaves. Divide in half, reserving 1 portion for basting and 1 for a sauce.

Arrange the veal on the grill rack. Grill over direct medium heat until done, about 20 minutes, basting with the Marsala sauce and turning with tongs once.

Arrange the peppers and endive on the grill basket. Place the basket on the grill rack and grill until hot and lightly browned, about 10 minutes, basting with the Marsala sauce and turning with tongs occasionally. Warm the remaining Marsala sauce on the stove top. Transfer the veal, peppers and endive to a serving platter, and drizzle the hot Marsala sauce over the veal and vegetables. Serve immediately.

HELPFUL HINT

Trim visible fat to reduce flare-ups.

PER SERVING:
Calories: 226
Fat (g): 7.3
Saturated Fat (g): 3.2
Cholesterol (mg): 74
Carbohydrates (g): 12.4
Sodium (mg): 154
Dietary Fiber (g): 4.4

WARM SEA SCALLOP SALAD WITH MESCLUN

Long used in Europe, mesclun is simply a potpourri of young salad greens and can include arugula, dandelion, frisée, mâche and sorrel. Slightly bitter, mesclun contrasts nicely with the aniselike fennel and tart grapefruit flavors in this unique dish.

PREPARATION TIME:
10 to 15 minutes
COOKING TIME:
10 to 15 minutes
SERVINGS: *4*

1	pound sea scallops
2	teaspoons olive oil
1	ruby red grapefruit, peeled and cut into wedges
2	fennel bulbs, trimmed and quartered
4	plum tomatoes
4	cups mesclun greens
2	cups garlic croutons
2	tablespoons fat-free or light bleu cheese dressing

PER SERVING:
Calories: 245
Fat (g): 4.6
Saturated Fat (g): 0.7
Cholesterol (mg): 37
Carbohydrates (g): 28
Sodium (mg): 387
Dietary Fiber (g): 4.9

Preheat the grill and place a grill rack on the grill. Coat a grill basket or topper with cooking spray. Place the scallops and oil in a self-sealing plastic bag, turning to coat the scallops with the oil. Arrange the scallops, grapefruit, fennel and tomatoes in the grill basket. Grill over direct medium heat until the scallops are cooked through and the vegetables are hot, 10 to 15 minutes, turning with tongs once. Transfer to a clean work surface.

Cut the core from the fennel; discard the core. Slice the tomatoes. Divide the mesclun among 4 salad plates or bowls. Top with the scallops, grapefruit, fennel, tomatoes and croutons. Drizzle the bleu dressing over the salad.

HELPFUL HINTS

Cutting the grapefruit into wedges is quick and easy. But if you prefer to peel and section it, feel free to do so.

Leave the core attached to the fennel wedges until after cooking. Otherwise, the wedges will come apart, and you'll have more pieces to turn and take off the grill.

LOBSTER BAKE

One of summer's pleasures: A classic cookout sporting rosemary-infused potatoes, chive-and-cheese-dusted corn on the cob, balsamic-marinated tomatoes and Neptune's specialty—lobster tails. Each component is easy to make and can be doubled, tripled and more to feed a crowd.

MENU

Rosemary Potatoes

Cob Corn with Chives and Cheese

Grilled Tomatoes Marinated in Balsamic Vinegar

Lobster Tails with Lemon-Butter

Rosemary Potatoes

1	teaspoons olive oil
1/4	cup cider vinegar
1	tablespoon minced fresh rosemary
2	teaspoons Dijon mustard
1/2	teaspoon sugar
4	Yukon-Gold or russet potatoes (about 1 pound)

Whisk the oil, vinegar, rosemary, mustard and sugar in a small bowl until well combined. Microwave the potatoes until almost done, 5 to 8 minutes. Cut in half and place in a medium-size bowl. Pour in the rosemary-mustard mixture; toss to coat. Marinate, covered, at room temperature for 30 to 60 minutes, turning occasionally.

Preheat the grill. Coat a grill rack with cooking spray; place on the grill. Arrange the potatoes on the grill rack. Grill over indirect medium heat until hot and golden brown, 5 to 10 minutes, turning occasionally.

HELPFUL HINT

If the potatoes are quite large, quarter them so they soak up more of the rosemary-mustard vinaigrette.

PREPARATION TIME:
5 to 10 minutes plus marinating
COOKING TIME:
10 to 20 minutes
SERVINGS: *4*

PER SERVING:
Calories: 113
Fat (g): 1.3
Saturated Fat (g): 0.2
Cholesterol (mg): 0
Carbohydrates (g): 24
Sodium (mg): 13
Dietary Fiber (g): 2.1

Cob Corn with Chives and Cheese

Butter-flavored cooking spray

4 ears corn on the cob

1 tablespoon grated Romano cheese

$^1/_4$ cup minced fresh chives

PREPARATION TIME:

5 minutes

COOKING TIME:

10 to 15 minutes

SERVINGS: **4**

Preheat the grill. Coat a grill rack with cooking spray; place it on the grill. Cut four 12-inch squares of foil. Mist the corn with the cooking spray and place 1 ear in the center of a foil square. Sprinkle $^1/_4$ tablespoon Romano cheese and 1 tablespoon chives over each ear. Bring up the sides of the foil and fold to seal. Arrange on the grill rack.

Grill over direct medium heat until tender and hot, about 10 to 15 minutes, turning with tongs several times.

HELPFUL HINT

For maximum flavor, use freshly grated Romano cheese; for maximum convenience, use the pre-grated variety.

PER SERVING:
Calories: 65
Fat (g): 0.9
Saturated Fat (g): 0.3
Cholesterol (mg): 1
Carbohydrates (g): 14.3
Sodium (mg): 26
Dietary Fiber (g): 1.8

Grilled Tomatoes Marinated in Balsamic Vinegar

$^1/_4$ cup balsamic vinegar

1 teaspoon olive oil

2 tablespoons minced fresh basil

$^1/_2$ teaspoon sugar

2 large tomatoes, seeded and cut into wedges (about 1 pound)

Preheat the grill and place a grill rack on the grill. Coat a grill topper, wok or basket with cooking spray. Whisk the vinegar, oil, basil and sugar in a medium-size bowl until well mixed. Arrange the tomatoes on the grill. Grill until hot, about 5 minutes, carefully turning with tongs once. Transfer to the bowl with the vinegar-basil mixture. Toss very gently to coat well. Let marinate at room temperature for 30 to 45 minutes.

HELPFUL HINT

Select slightly firm, meaty tomatoes for this recipe.

PREPARATION TIME:

6 minutes plus marinating

COOKING TIME:

5 minutes

SERVINGS: *4*

PER SERVING:
Calories: 56
Fat (g): 1.5
Saturated Fat (g): 0.2
Cholesterol (mg): 0
Carbohydrates (g): 10
Sodium (mg): 13
Dietary Fiber (g): 1.3

Lobster Tails with Lemon-Butter

1 tablespoon pickling spice
4 lobster tails
2 tablespoons lemon juice
2 tablespoons melted whipped butter
1 tablespoon minced fresh dill

PREPARATION TIME:
5 to 10 minutes
COOKING TIME:
10 to 15 minutes
SERVINGS: *4*

Place the pickling spice in a mesh tea ball or tie it in cheesecloth. Fill a large pot with water and bring to a boil; add the pickling spice and lobster tails. Cook just until done, about 10 minutes; drain. Discard the spice. Transfer to a work surface and, using kitchen shears, cut away the membrane on the underside of each tail.

Preheat the grill. Coat a grill rack with cooking spray; place on the grill. Combine the lemon juice, butter and dill. Arrange the lobster, shell side down, on the grill rack. Grill until hot, about 5 minutes, brushing liberally and often with the lemon-butter mixture.

HELPFUL HINT

Lobster tails tend to curl as they cook. Force them to lie as flat as possible on the grill for brushing the meat with lemon-butter.

PER SERVING:
Calories: 184
Fat (g): 6
Saturated Fat (g): 3
Cholesterol (mg): 107
Carbohydrates (g): 3.2
Sodium (mg): 501
Dietary Fiber (g): 0.4

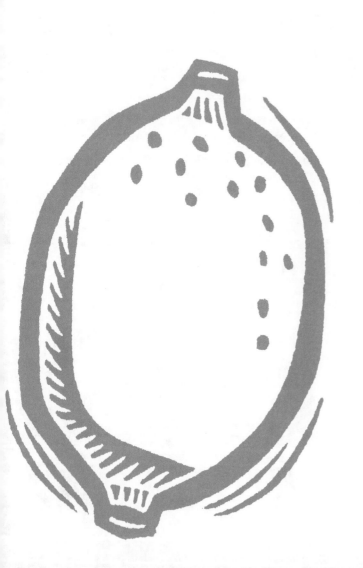

quick ignition dishes

Chicken Breasts with Honey-Curry Rub

Cumin-Seasoned Pork Chops

Fast Barbecue Turkey Tenders

Filet Mignon with Mustard Seeds

Garlic-Lemon Steak

Salmon Fillet with Tarragon

Tarragon-Orange Chicken

CHICKEN BREASTS WITH HONEY-CURRY RUB

Ready ... set ... grill! This dish with its flavorful yogurt-based rub comes together in no time flat. And delectable honey smoothes curry's pungent edges. Rice and lightly steamed peas make perfect serve-withs.

PREPARATION TIME:

5 minutes

COOKING TIME:

15 to 20 minutes

SERVINGS: **4**

¼	cup plain nonfat yogurt
2	teaspoons cornstarch
2	teaspoons Dijon mustard
2	teaspoons honey
¾	teaspoon curry powder
1	pound skinless, boneless chicken breasts

Preheat the grill. Coat a grill rack with cooking spray; place on the grill. Whisk the yogurt, cornstarch, mustard, honey and curry in a small bowl until well combined. Spread over both sides of the chicken. Arrange on the grill rack.

Grill over indirect medium heat until done throughout and the juices run clear, 15 to 20 minutes, turning with a spatula or tongs once.

HELPFUL HINT

This moist rub spreads nicely with either a brush or spatula. Slather it on thickly for best results.

PER SERVING:
Calories: 214
Fat (g): 4.3
Saturated Fat (g): 1.2
Cholesterol (mg): 97
Carbohydrates (g): 5.7
Sodium (mg): 109
Dietary Fiber (g): 0.2

CUMIN-SEASONED PORK CHOPS

When dinner hour is rush hour, serve up this super-speedy dish. The thick, rich paste of sour cream and earthy seasonings takes less than 5 minutes to prepare and slather over the chops. Cooking is grill-fast.

PREPARATION TIME:

5 minutes

COOKING TIME:

20 minutes

SERVINGS: **4**

$1/4$ cup fat-free sour cream

1   teaspoon ground cumin

$1/2$ teaspoon dried marjoram leaves

$1/4$ teaspoon freshly ground black pepper

$3/4$ pound center-cut loin pork chops

Preheat the grill. Coat a grill rack with cooking spray; place on the grill. Whisk the sour cream, cumin, marjoram and pepper until well combined. Using a metal spatula, spread over both sides of the pork. Arrange on the grill rack.

Grill over indirect medium heat until cooked throughout, about 20 minutes, turning with a spatula or tongs once. Serve immediately.

HELPFUL HINT

Score the fat along the edges of the chops or they may curl during cooking.

PER SERVING:
Calories: 249
Fat (g): 9.3
Saturated Fat (g): 3.3
Cholesterol (mg): 93
Carbohydrates (g): 3.3
Sodium (mg): 82
Dietary Fiber (g): 0.3

FAST BARBECUE TURKEY TENDERS

When you're looking for a barbecue sauce that's quick to make and a little (but not too) different from the usual ketchup-based sauce, try this one. It starts with chili sauce and gets its zip from mustard and hot-pepper sauce. Brown sugar provides a touch of sweetness.

$\frac{1}{4}$ cup chili sauce

1 teaspoon mustard powder

1 teaspoon light brown sugar

$\frac{1}{4}$ teaspoon hot-pepper sauce

1 turkey tenderloin (about $\frac{3}{4}$ pound)

Preheat the grill. Coat a grill rack with cooking spray; place on the grill. Combine the chili sauce, mustard powder, brown sugar and hot-pepper sauce in a small bowl, stirring to mix well. With a brush, paint the turkey on both sides with the chili sauce mix. Arrange on the grill rack.

Grill over indirect medium heat until cooked throughout and juices run clear, about 25 to 35 minutes, turning with a spatula or tongs once. Slice thinly and serve.

HELPFUL HINT

Each brand of chili sauce has its own unique flavor. Experiment until you find your favorite.

PREPARATION TIME:
5 minutes
COOKING TIME:
25 to 35 minutes
SERVINGS: **4**

PER SERVING:
Calories: 162
Fat (g): 4.4
Saturated Fat (g): 1.4
Cholesterol (mg): 67
Carbohydrates (g): 4.5
Sodium (mg): 59
Dietary Fiber (g): 0

103

FILET MIGNON WITH MUSTARD SEEDS

Here's superbly grilled filet mignon at its very best: topped with a fast and nippy crust of celery seeds, coarsely ground pepper and mustard seeds. I think you'll agree—it's delectable.

PREPARATION TIME:

5 minutes

COOKING TIME:

10 to 20 minutes

SERVINGS: **4**

$1/4$ teaspoon celery seeds
$1/2$ teaspoon freshly ground black pepper
1 teaspoon yellow mustard seeds
1 tablespoon steak sauce
4 filet mignon steaks (about $3/4$ pound total)

Preheat the grill. Coat a grill rack with cooking spray; place on the grill. Thoroughly mix the celery seeds, pepper, mustard seeds and steak sauce in a small bowl. Rub the mixture over both sides of the filet mignon, pressing the seeds into the meat. Arrange on the grill rack.

Grill over indirect medium heat to the desired doneness, 10 to 20 minutes, turning with a spatula or tongs once. Slice thinly and serve.

HELPFUL HINT

Yellow mustard seeds are easier to find than black seeds. But if you have access to the black variety, use a combination of the black and yellow.

PER SERVING:
Calories: 160
Fat (g): 5.1
Saturated Fat (g): 1.9
Cholesterol (mg): 76
Carbohydrates (g): 0.8
Sodium (mg): 110
Dietary Fiber (g): 0.2

GARLIC-LEMON STEAK

Lemon and garlic—both are equally assertive in this extra-easy and extra-fast rub that deliciously flavors sirloin steak.

2	large cloves garlic, crushed
2	teaspoons grated lemon peel
1	teaspoon dried thyme leaves
1	teaspoon olive oil
3/4	pound beef sirloin steak, trimmed of visible fat

Preheat the grill. Coat a grill rack with cooking spray; place on the grill. Mix the garlic, lemon peel, thyme and oil in a small bowl until well combined. Rub over both sides of the beef steak. Arrange on the grill rack.

Grill over indirect medium heat to the desired doneness, 10 to 20 minutes, turning with a spatula or tongs once. Slice thinly and serve.

HELPFUL HINTS

For maximum lemon flavor without bitterness, grate only the deeply colored part of the lemon peel. The white part, or pith, contains the bitter elements.

Remember to trim the steak of excess fat to prevent flaring.

PREPARATION TIME:
5 minutes
COOKING TIME:
10 to 20 minutes
SERVINGS: **4**

PER SERVING:
Calories: 171
Fat (g): 6.8
Saturated Fat (g): 1.9
Cholesterol (mg): 56
Carbohydrates (g): 0.9
Sodium (mg): 56
Dietary Fiber (g): 0.2

SALMON FILLET WITH TARRAGON

Tarragon's assertiveness is well matched with garlic, mustard and salmon in this exceptional yet easy recipe. Here, I've used a salmon fillet, but you can substitute a steak. Just be sure to rub the seasoning mixtures on both sides of the salmon and to turn the steak once during grilling.

PREPARATION TIME:
5 minutes
COOKING TIME:
20 to 30 minutes
SERVINGS: **4**

2	teaspoons lemon juice
2	teaspoons Dijon mustard
1	pound salmon fillet
1½	teaspoons dried tarragon
2	cloves garlic, minced

Preheat the grill. Coat a grill rack with cooking spray; place on the grill. Whisk the lemon juice and mustard in a small bowl. Spread over the salmon flesh. Sprinkle the tarragon and garlic over the lemon-mustard mixture. Arrange on the grill rack.

Grill over indirect medium heat until done and the fish flakes when gently probed with the tip of a sharp knife, 20 to 30 minutes.

HELPFUL HINTS

To bring out dried tarragon's flavor, crush the leaves between your fingers before sprinkling them over the salmon.

For super-quick prep, use bottled lemon juice and pre-minced garlic.

PER SERVING:
Calories: 173
Fat (g): 7
Saturated Fat (g): 1.5
Cholesterol (mg): 51
Carbohydrates (g): 1.3
Sodium (mg): 67
Dietary Fiber (g): 0.1

TARRAGON-ORANGE CHICKEN

Give juicy chicken plenty of appeal with this citrusy rub. It goes together in minutes and can be used on skinless drumsticks or thighs as well as the breasts.

PREPARATION TIME:
5 minutes
COOKING TIME:
15 to 20 minutes
SERVINGS: **4**

- 1/4 teaspoon freshly ground black pepper
- 1 teaspoon dried tarragon
- 1 teaspoon grated orange peel
- 2 teaspoons olive oil
- 1 pound skinless, boneless chicken breasts

Preheat the grill. Coat a grill rack with cooking spray; place on the grill. Mix the pepper, tarragon and orange peel in a small bowl until well combined. Rub the oil over both sides of the chicken. Rub on the tarragon-orange mixture. Arrange the chicken on the grill rack.

Grill over indirect medium heat until the chicken is cooked throughout and the juices run clear, about 15 to 20 minutes, turning once with a spatula or tongs.

PER SERVING:
Calories: 208
Fat (g): 6.3
Saturated Fat (g): 1.5
Cholesterol (mg): 96
Carbohydrates (g): 0.4
Sodium (mg): 84
Dietary Fiber (g): 0.1

better

sa

burgers & special ndwiches

Basil and Mozzarella Burgers

California Burgers with Black Olives

Lamb Patties Stuffed with Feta

Spicy Veal Burgers with Sauerkraut

Teriyaki Burgers

Tex-Mex Burgers

Traditional Burgers with Barbecue Sauce

Turkey and Cranberry Burgers

Breakfast Sandwiches with Canadian Bacon and Bleu Cheese

Crisp Nachos

Eggplant Club with Tomatoes and Feta

Grilled Ham and Cheese on Rye

Grilled Italian Bread with Sun-Dried Tomatoes

Lamb Tortilla Packets

Pepperoni and Pepperoncini Pizza

Quick Pinto Bean Burritos

Red Onion and Pepper Focaccia

Thymely Chicken in Pita Pockets

Sweet Sausage Sandwiches

better burgers and special sandwiches

BASIL AND MOZZARELLA BURGERS

If the Italians had invented the burger, it would be this one. Garlic, pepperoni, mozzarella cheese, pepperoncini (pickled chilies, which are also called Tuscan peppers) and basil provide the Italian accent. Beef sirloin and onions form the base. When you're ready to grill some up, be sure to grab a fresh loaf of crusty Italian bread. For these burgers, it beats the usual roll.

PREPARATION TIME:

20 minutes

COOKING TIME:

20 minutes

SERVINGS: **4**

$3/4$	pound ground beef sirloin
$3/4$	cup cooked couscous
$3/4$	cup finely chopped onions
1	egg white
3	cloves garlic, minced
1	tablespoon minced fresh parsley
4	very thin slices pepperoni, minced
4	thin slices mozzarella cheese
8	slices lightly toasted Italian bread
$1/2$	cup crushed tomatoes, warmed
8	basil leaves
4	pepperoncini

Preheat the grill. Coat a grill rack with cooking spray; place on the grill.

Combine the beef, couscous, onions, egg white, garlic, parsley and pepperoni in a large bowl; mix gently but thoroughly. Shape into 4 patties, each $3\frac{1}{2}$ to 4 inches in diameter. Arrange on the grill rack.

Grill over indirect medium heat until done, 8 to 10 minutes per side, turning once with a spatula and topping with the mozzarella during the last 3 minutes of cooking. Place the patties on 4 toasted Italian bread slices; top with the crushed tomatoes, basil, pepperoncini, and remaining bread slices.

HELPFUL HINT

To cook enough couscous for this recipe: Bring $3/4$ cup water to a boil in a 2-quart saucepan. Stir in $1/4$ cup plus 2 tablespoons couscous. Cover and remove from the heat. Let stand for 5 minutes. Fluff with a fork.

PER SERVING:
Calories: 348
Fat (g): 9
Saturated Fat (g): 3.9
Cholesterol (mg): 71
Carbohydrates (g): 28.9
Sodium (mg): 546
Dietary Fiber (g): 2.4

CALIFORNIA BURGERS WITH BLACK OLIVES

It was just yesterday, wasn't it? when California burgers were all the rage. Though not unique anymore, they're still a favorite among burger aficionados, including me. These boast hot-pepper sauce, black olives and mustard and are topped with fresh ripe tomato and cucumber as well as red onion and red leaf lettuce. They're pleasantly different and delicious.

PREPARATION TIME:
10 minutes

COOKING TIME:
20 minutes

SERVINGS: *4*

PER SERVING:
Calories: 379
Fat (g): 8.3
Saturated Fat (g): 2.4
Cholesterol (mg): 61
Carbohydrates (g): 40
Sodium (mg): 483
Dietary Fiber (g): 3.2

$^3/_4$ pound ground beef sirloin

$^3/_4$ cup finely chopped soft rye bread crumbs

$^3/_4$ cup finely chopped onions

1 egg white

4 black olives, finely chopped

$^3/_4$ teaspoon hot-pepper sauce

$^3/_4$ teaspoon prepared mustard

4 crusty rolls, split

4 slices tomato

4 slices red onion

4 leaves red leaf lettuce

4 thin slices cucumber

Preheat the grill. Coat a grill rack with cooking spray; place on the grill.

Combine the beef, bread crumbs, onions, egg white, olives, hot-pepper sauce and mustard in a large bowl; mix gently but thoroughly. Shape into 4 patties, each $3^1/_2$ to 4 inches in diameter. Arrange on the grill rack.

Grill over indirect medium heat until done, 5 to 7 minutes per side, turning with a spatula once. Arrange the rolls on the grill, cut sides down; toast for 3 minutes. Place the patties in the rolls and top with the tomatoes, onions, lettuce and cucumber.

HELPFUL HINTS

Two small pieces of bread will equal about $^3/_4$ cup soft crumbs. Use a mini food processor to chop the crumbs finely.

Peel the cucumber only if it has been waxed.

LAMB PATTIES STUFFED WITH FETA

There's a surprise tucked inside each of these delectable meat packets: a chunk of creamy-white, tangy feta cheese—a prized Greek cheese. The patties themselves sport lemon peel, tomato, cinnamon and pepper. For a spirited garnish, top each with mint leaves.

PREPARATION TIME:
10 minutes
COOKING TIME:
20 minutes
SERVINGS: **4**

1/2	pound lean ground lamb
3/4	cup fine soft bread crumbs
3/4	cup finely chopped onions
1	egg white
1	tablespoon tomato paste
1	teaspoon grated lemon peel
1/2	teaspoon cinnamon
1/2	teaspoon freshly ground black pepper
2	ounces feta cheese, cut into 4 pieces
4	English muffins, split
	Mint leaves

Preheat the grill. Coat a grill rack with cooking spray; place on the grill.

Combine the lamb, bread crumbs, onions, egg white, tomato paste, lemon peel, cinnamon and black pepper in a large bowl; mix gently but thoroughly. Shape into four 3- to 3½-inch patties, tucking a piece of feta in the center of each. Arrange on the grill rack.

Grill the patties over direct medium heat until done, 8 to 10 minutes per side, turning once with a spatula. Arrange the English muffins on the grill, cut sides down; toast for 3 minutes. Garnish with the mint leaves.

HELPFUL HINT

Use a mini food processor to finely chop the onions. Patties made with coarsely chopped onions may fall apart during cooking.

PER SERVING:
Calories: 319
Fat (g): 8.7
Saturated Fat (g): 3.9
Cholesterol (mg): 64
Carbohydrates (g): 34.7
Sodium (mg): 525
Dietary Fiber (g): 2.7

SPICY VEAL BURGERS WITH SAUERKRAUT

Got a yen for sauerkraut and mashed potatoes seasoned with nutmeg, cloves, ginger—hallmarks of hearty German cuisine? Find them all here in sassy burgers that will please your palate—and a ravenous appetite.

PREPARATION TIME:

20 minutes

COOKING TIME:

20 minutes

SERVINGS: **4**

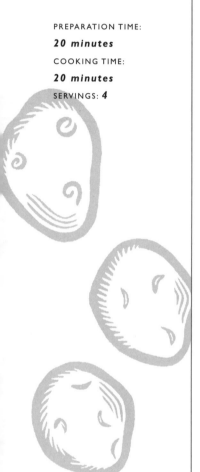

$1/4$	cup fat-free beef broth
2	tablespoons dry red wine
$3/4$	teaspoon pickling spice
2	tablespoons fine gingersnap crumbs (about 2 cookies)
2	tablespoons nonfat sour cream
$3/4$	pound ground veal
$3/4$	cup mashed potatoes
$1/4$	cup finely chopped onions
1	egg white
$1/8$	teaspoon ground cloves
$1/2$	teaspoon nutmeg
4	wheat Kaiser rolls, split
$1/4$	cup sauerkraut, rinsed, drained and warmed

Whisk the beef broth, red wine and pickling spice in a small saucepan until well combined. Bring to a boil over medium-high heat; reduce the heat and simmer gently for 5 minutes. Strain the liquid into a bowl and discard the spices. Return the liquid to the pot. Stir in the gingersnaps and sour cream. Keep warm, covered, over very low heat.

Preheat the grill. Coat a grill rack with cooking spray; place on the grill.

Combine the veal, potatoes, onions, egg white, cloves and nutmeg in a large bowl; mix gently but thoroughly. Shape into 4 patties, each $3^1/2$ to 4 inches in diameter. Arrange on the grill rack.

Grill over indirect medium heat until done, 8 to 10 minutes per side, turning once with a spatula. Arrange the rolls on the grill, cut sides down; toast for 3 minutes. Place the patties in the rolls and top with the gingersnap-sour-cream mixture and sauerkraut.

HELPFUL HINTS

For a quick mashed potato, microwave a medium-size russet on High until very tender. Peel. Mash in a small bowl, using a potato masher and adding milk for a creamy but stiff consistency.

Rinse the sauerkraut under cool water for 2 to 3 minutes to reduce sodium levels; drain.

PER SERVING:
Calories: 355
Fat (g): 7.8
Saturated Fat (g): 1.9
Cholesterol (mg): 56
Carbohydrates (g): 45
Sodium (mg): 616
Dietary Fiber (g): 2.2

TERIYAKI BURGERS

Looking for a unique, updated burger—one bursting with tantalizing flavors? Search no more. This Asian turkey version is seasoned with teriyaki sauce, garlic, gingerroot and sherry. After grilling, each bundle of flavor is tucked between slices of hearty whole grain bread and topped with alfalfa sprouts and lightly steamed asparagus spears. Simple. Elegant.

PREPARATION TIME:

20 minutes

COOKING TIME:

20 minutes

SERVINGS: **4**

2	tablespoons low-sodium teriyaki
4	cloves garlic, minced
1	tablespoon minced gingerroot
1	tablespoon sherry
1	teaspoon sugar
$\frac{3}{4}$	pound ground turkey breast
$\frac{3}{4}$	cup cooked rice
1	egg white
8	slices whole grain bread, toasted
1	cup alfalfa sprouts
4	asparagus spears, steamed and cut into 2-inch slices
	Duck sauce (optional)

PER SERVING:
Calories: 328
Fat (g): 1.9
Saturated Fat (g): 0.3
Cholesterol (mg): 71
Carbohydrates (g): 46
Sodium (mg): 500
Dietary Fiber (g): 6.7

Whisk the teriyaki, garlic, gingerroot, sherry and sugar in a small bowl until well mixed. Preheat the grill. Coat a grill rack with cooking spray; place on the grill.

Combine the turkey, rice, egg white and teriyaki mixture in a large bowl; mix gently but thoroughly. Shape into 4 patties, each $3\frac{1}{2}$ to 4 inches in diameter. Arrange on the grill rack.

Grill over indirect medium heat until done, 8 to 10 minutes per side, turning with a spatula once. Place on 4 toasted bread slices; top with the sprouts, asparagus and remaining bread slices. Serve with duck sauce if desired.

HELPFUL HINT

Make *firm* patties; loose ones will break apart and fall through the grill rack.

TEX-MEX BURGERS

Experience taco flavors in the shape of a patty, in a roll. Seriously. These burgers have the character of home-style tacos—thanks to lean beef, sweet peppers, pungent chili powder, tomato salsa, Monterey Jack cheese with jalapeños and even cilantro. Be prepared to make them often; they're very tasty.

PREPARATION TIME:

15 minutes

COOKING TIME:

20 minutes

SERVINGS: *4*

³⁄₄	pound ground beef sirloin
³⁄₄	cup crushed baked (fat-free) tortilla chips (about 20 chips)
¹⁄₃	cup finely chopped onions
¹⁄₃	cup finely chopped green sweet peppers
1	egg white
2	teaspoons chili powder
3	cloves garlic, minced
4	thin slices Monterey Jack cheese with jalapeños
4	crusty rolls, split
¹⁄₂	cup medium-hot salsa
1	bunch cilantro

Preheat the grill. Coat a grill rack with cooking spray; place on the grill.

Combine the beef, crushed tortilla chips, onions, sweet peppers, egg white, chili powder and garlic in a large bowl; mix gently but thoroughly. Shape into 4 patties, each 3¹⁄₂ to 4 inches in diameter. Arrange on the grill rack.

Grill over indirect medium heat until done, 8 to 10 minutes per side, turning once with a spatula and topping with the Monterey Jack cheese during the last 3 minutes of cooking. Arrange the rolls on the grill, cut sides down; toast for 3 minutes. Place the patties in the rolls and top with the salsa and cilantro.

PER SERVING:
Calories: 407
Fat (g): 9.9
Saturated Fat (g): 3.6
Cholesterol (mg): 68
Carbohydrates (g): 41
Sodium (mg): 568
Dietary Fiber (g): 3.4

TRADITIONAL BURGERS WITH BARBECUE SAUCE

Forget ketchup and pickle relish. These sizzling burgers need neither because they're accompanied by a superb mesquite barbecue sauce that cooks on the grill and packs a ton of flavor. Soft bread crumbs and finely chopped onions keep the burgers themselves moist and tasty.

PREPARATION TIME:

15 minutes

COOKING TIME:

20 minutes

SERVINGS: **4**

- $^1\!/_2$ cup no-salt-added tomato sauce
- 2 tablespoons molasses
- 2 teaspoons red wine vinegar
- 1 tablespoon mustard
- 2 teaspoons mesquite liquid smoke
- 2 teaspoons minced dried onions
- $^3\!/_4$ pound ground sirloin
- $^1\!/_2$ cup fine soft bread crumbs
- 1 egg white
- $^1\!/_2$ cup finely chopped onions
- $^1\!/_2$ teaspoon freshly ground black pepper
- 4 hamburger buns, split

Whisk the tomato sauce, molasses, red wine vinegar, mustard, liquid smoke and dried onions in a small saucepan until well mixed.

Preheat the grill. Coat a grill rack with cooking spray; place on the grill. Combine the sirloin, bread crumbs, egg white, chopped onions and pepper in a large bowl; mix gently but thoroughly. Shape into 4 patties, each $3^1\!/_2$ to 4 inches in diameter. Arrange on the grill rack.

Grill over indirect medium heat until done, 8 to 10 minutes per side, turning once with a spatula. Place the saucepan with the tomato sauce mixture on the grill. Heat until the sauce is hot, about 5 minutes, stirring frequently. Spoon a small amount onto each patty.

Arrange the rolls on the grill, cut sides down; toast for 2 to 3 minutes. Place the patties in the rolls and top with more sauce. Serve immediately.

HELPFUL HINT

If the handle on your saucepan isn't heat proof (or you're not sure), wrap it in several layers of foil before placing the pan on the grill.

PER SERVING:
Calories: 344
Fat (g): 7.5
Saturated Fat (g): 2.5
Cholesterol (mg): 61
Carbohydrates (g): 36
Sodium (mg): 360
Dietary Fiber (g): 2.3

TURKEY AND CRANBERRY BURGERS

Why wait 'til the holidays for turkey and cranberries? With these no-hassle burgers, you can nosh on trim turkey (with a touch of sage), sweet-tart cranberries and seasoned stuffing year 'round. Egg white helps bind the burgers and keep them moist. A complete meal for a light lunch or supper.

PREPARATION TIME:

10 minutes

COOKING TIME:

20 minutes

SERVINGS: *4*

3/4 pound ground turkey breast

3/4 cup herb-seasoned bread stuffing

1/2 cup finely minced onions

1 egg white

1 tablespoon finely chopped fresh sage

1 teaspoon freshly ground black pepper

4 poppy seed Kaiser rolls, split

1/2 cup whole cranberry sauce

4 leaves red leaf lettuce

Preheat the grill. Coat a grill rack with cooking spray; place on the grill. Combine the turkey, bread stuffing, onions, egg white and sage in a large bowl; mix gently but thoroughly. Shape into 4 patties, each 3 to 3 1/2 inches in diameter. Rub about 1/8 teaspoon pepper over each side of each patty. Arrange on the grill rack.

Grill over indirect medium heat until done, 8 to 10 minutes per side, turning with a spatula once. Arrange the rolls on the grill, cut sides down; toast for 2 to 3 minutes. Place the patties in the rolls and top with cranberries and lettuce. Serve immediately.

HELPFUL HINT

Jellied cranberries can replace the whole cranberry sauce if you wish. Or you could use a special homemade sauce.

PER SERVING:
Calories: 382
Fat (g): 3.6
Saturated Fat (g): 0.6
Cholesterol (mg): 71
Carbohydrates (g): 52
Sodium (mg): 472
Dietary Fiber (g): 2.9

BREAKFAST SANDWICHES WITH CANADIAN BACON AND BLEU CHEESE

PREPARATION TIME:

10 minutes

COOKING TIME:

10 minutes

SERVINGS: *4*

Grilling isn't just for dinner fare anymore. It's for breakfast, brunch, lunch. . . anytime. As are these fast-to-fix sandwiches of lean Canadian bacon, juicy Bartlett pears, tangy bleu cheese, pungent sorrel and sweet Spanish onion on traditional English muffins. Use spinach instead of sorrel if you want.

8   slices Canadian bacon ($\frac{1}{2}$ ounce each)
4   slices white Spanish onion (1 ounce each)
2   small Bartlett pears, halved and cored
4   English muffins, split
1   teaspoon horseradish mustard
2   ounces bleu cheese, crumbled
8   sorrel leaves

Preheat the grill and place a grill rack on the grill. Coat a grill basket or topper with cooking spray. Arrange the Canadian bacon, onion, and pears in the basket. Grill over direct medium heat until hot, about 4 minutes, turning with tongs once. Transfer to a platter.

Arrange the English muffins, cut sides down, on the grill rack. Grill until lightly toasted, about 2 minutes. Using tongs or hot mitts, transfer to a work surface. Spread the mustard over the cut sides. Top with the bleu cheese. Arrange, cut sides up, on the grill rack. Grill for 1 minute. Transfer to a work surface.

Layer the bacon, onion, pears and sorrel on the muffin bottoms, starting and ending with the bacon. Top with the muffin tops.

HELPFUL HINT

Use pears that are slightly crisp; ripe ones will soften too quickly.

PER SERVING:
Calories: 249
Fat (g): 6.4
Saturated Fat (g): 3.8
Cholesterol (mg): 26
Carbohydrates (g): 37.8
Sodium (mg): 798
Dietary Fiber (g): 4

CRISP NACHOS

Nachos are nachos, right? Well, not quite, as you'll discover when you snack on these. They're spicy and special with just the right combination of Tex-Mex-style heat, crispy chips and fresh ingredients: tomatoes, scallions, Monterey Jack cheese with jalapeños and cilantro. Buen apetito!

PREPARATION TIME:

10 minutes

COOKING TIME:

5 minutes

SERVINGS: *4*

24	baked (fat-free) tortilla chips
3	plum tomatoes, minced
6	scallions, minced
½	cup shredded Monterey Jack cheese with jalapeños
¼	teaspoon dried cilantro
¼	teaspoon chili powder

Preheat the grill and place a grill rack on the grill. Coat a grill basket or topper with cooking spray.

Arrange the tortilla chips in the basket. Sprinkle the tomatoes, scallions and Monterey Jack cheese evenly over the chips. Top with the cilantro and chili powder.

Grill just until the cheese melts, 3 to 5 minutes.

HELPFUL HINT

If the tomatoes are juicy, seed them before mincing. To seed, cut the tomatoes in half crosswise and gently squeeze out the seeds and juice.

PER SERVING (6 CHIPS):

Calories: 69
Fat (g): 2.7
Saturated Fat (g): 1.3
Cholesterol (mg): 7.5
Carbohydrates (g): 9
Sodium (mg): 102
Dietary Fiber (g): 1.2

EGGPLANT CLUB WITH TOMATOES AND FETA

The venerable club gets a complete makeover in this fresh vegetable sandwich. Gone are the meat and rich mayonnaise dressing. In their places are eggplant, tomatoes, basil, nonfat yogurt and feta cheese. A smidgen of Caesar salad dressing punches up flavor even more. Whether to peel the eggplant is a personal decision; I like to leave the skin on, but some cooks think it has a bitter taste.

PREPARATION TIME:

15 minutes

COOKING TIME:

15 minutes

SERVINGS: **4**

1	tablespoon Caesar salad dressing
1	small eggplant, cut into 16 thin slices
4	wheat Kaiser rolls, split
$\frac{1}{4}$	cup plain nonfat yogurt
1	large tomato, cut into 8 thin slices
$\frac{1}{2}$	medium red onion, cut into 4 thin slices
8	basil leaves, finely chopped
2	ounces feta cheese, finely crumbled
4	leaves romaine lettuce

Preheat the grill. Coat a grill rack with cooking spray; place on the grill. Drizzle or lightly brush the Caesar salad dressing over 1 side of each eggplant slice. Arrange the slices, dressing side up, on the grill rack.

Grill over direct medium heat just until lightly browned on the bottom, juicy on the top and tender, about 15 minutes. Arrange the rolls, cut sides down, on the grill; toast for 3 minutes. Using a spatula or tongs, remove to a platter. Spread the yogurt on the cut sides of the rolls.

Layer the eggplant, tomato, onion, basil and feta cheese on half of the roll, starting and ending with the eggplant. Top with the lettuce and remaining roll. Serve sandwiches immediately.

HELPFUL HINT

Judging when eggplant is done is tricky, so err toward undercooking if in doubt. Remember, you can always return the slices to the grill for a minute or two.

PER SERVING:
Calories: 266
Fat (g): 8
Saturated Fat (g): 2.9
Cholesterol (mg): 13
Carbohydrates (g): 39
Sodium (mg): 530
Dietary Fiber (g): 3.7

GRILLED HAM AND CHEESE ON RYE

Remember those comforting grilled cheese sandwiches of childhood? Here's a grown-up version. These quick throw-togethers include tangy mustard, red onion, juicy tomatoes, ham and sharp cheddar—all on rye. For a complete meal, serve with a beverage and piece of fresh fruit.

4 slices reduced-sodium tavern ham ($\frac{1}{2}$ ounce each)

4 slices reduced-sodium sharp cheddar cheese ($\frac{1}{2}$ ounce each)

4 slices red onion

8 thin tomato slices

8 slices Jewish rye bread

4 teaspoons horseradish mustard

Butter-flavored cooking spray

Preheat the grill. Coat a grill rack with cooking spray; place on the grill.

Layer the ham, cheese, onion and tomato on 4 bread slices. Top with the remaining bread. Spread $\frac{1}{2}$ teaspoon mustard over the outside of each sandwich; mist with the butter-flavored cooking spray.

Arrange on the grill rack. Grill until golden brown on each side, about 5 minutes a side, carefully turning with a spatula once.

HELPFUL HINT

To turn the sandwiches without the contents falling out, remove them from the grill. Then holding them in both hands, flip so the uncooked side is down. Slide with a spatula onto the grill rack.

PREPARATION TIME:

10 minutes

COOKING TIME:

10 minutes

SERVINGS: *4*

PER SERVING:
Calories: 244
Fat (g): 5.7
Saturated Fat (g): 2.2
Cholesterol (mg): 17
Carbohydrates (g): 36
Sodium (mg): 639
Dietary Fiber (g): 4.6

GRILLED ITALIAN BREAD WITH SUN-DRIED TOMATOES

PREPARATION TIME:

15 minutes

COOKING TIME:

5 to 10 minutes

SERVINGS: *4*

Who can resist this perennial favorite: Garlic bread, or bruschetta—which actually means "to roast over coals" in Italian? By itself, garlic bread is the perfect accompaniment for Italian-style salads, soups and pasta dishes. Used as a platform for savory toppings, it makes for stylishly delicious appetizers, snacks and side dishes. Here's how to make tomato-basil bruschetta (without the garlic) on the grill. It's as easy as toast.

2	tablespoons olive oil
1	loaf (1 pound) Italian bread, cut in half lengthwise
1/4	cup minced fresh parsley
2	tablespoons minced fresh basil
2	tablespoons finely chopped sun-dried tomatoes
1/4	cup grated Parmesan cheese

Preheat the grill. Coat a grill rack with cooking spray; place on the grill. Brush the olive oil over the cut sides of the bread. Arrange, cut sides down, on the grill rack. Grill over indirect medium heat until lightly toasted, 2 to 4 minutes.

Turn with tongs and sprinkle the parsley, basil, tomatoes and cheese over the toasted cut sides. Grill until lightly toasted on the uncut sides and the cheese is melted on the top, 2 to 4 minutes.

HELPFUL HINT

To keep calories and fat low, use sun-dried tomatoes that are not packed in oil.

PER SERVING:
Calories: 376
Fat (g): 10.9
Saturated Fat (g): 2.4
Cholesterol (mg): 3.5
Carbohydrates (g): 58.6
Sodium (mg): 349
Dietary Fiber (g): 2.7

LAMB TORTILLA PACKETS

Be a mealtime hero. Create a gyro (pronounced JEER-oh) taste-alike. It's easy to do. Simply season lean lamb with pepper and fragrant rosemary, then grill to perfection. Wrap it and a sauce of onion, cucumber, sour cream, tomatoes and feta cheese in a large tortilla. This gyro is relaxed enough for a weeknight yet special enough for company.

PREPARATION TIME:

20 minutes

COOKING TIME:

25 minutes

SERVINGS: **4**

$1/2$	cup nonfat sour cream
1	medium onion, chopped
1	small cucumber, peeled, seeded and diced
2	plum tomatoes, chopped
2	ounces feta cheese, crumbled
4	cloves garlic, crushed
12	fresh mint leaves, snipped (about 1 tablespoon)
$1/2$	pound lean lamb shoulder, trimmed of visible fat and cut into $3/4$-inch cubes
$1/2$	teaspoon olive oil
$1/4$	teaspoon freshly ground black pepper
1	teaspoon dried rosemary
4	flour tortillas, warmed (10-inch size)

Preheat the grill and place a grill rack on the grill. Coat a grill basket or topper with cooking spray. Gently mix the sour cream, onion, cucumber, tomatoes, feta cheese, garlic and mint in a medium-size bowl until well combined. In a small bowl, toss the lamb, oil, pepper and rosemary until well mixed.

Arrange the lamb in the basket or topper. Grill over direct medium heat for 10 minutes. Using tongs, turn. Grill until done, about 5 minutes more. Add to the sour cream mixture; toss gently to combine. Spread over the tortillas. Fold in opposite ends. Starting at 1 side, roll up jelly-roll fashion. Wrap each packet tightly in foil. Arrange on the grill. Heat over direct low heat until hot, about 10 minutes. Serve immediately.

HELPFUL HINT

Always warm tortillas according to package directions before using them. Why? Warming makes them pliable so they're less likely to crack and tear.

PER SERVING:
Calories: 322
Fat (g): 11.6
Saturated Fat (g): 4.7
Cholesterol (mg): 61
Carbohydrates (g): 30.9
Sodium (mg): 403
Dietary Fiber (g): 2.4

PEPPERONI AND PEPPERONCINI PIZZA

Faster than a delivery person can get to your door—this Italian pie is ready to eat. And it's a snap to make, thanks to preshredded mozzarella cheese and a store-bought crust. Pepperoni and pepperoncini pair up to top this pizza with special pizzazz. Your grill provides the essence of a wood-burning stove.

PREPARATION TIME:
15 minutes

COOKING TIME:
10 minutes

SERVINGS: *8*

1	prepared thin pizza crust (12-inch)
1	teaspoon olive oil
½	cup crushed tomatoes
2	ounces pepperoni, thinly sliced
2	ounces mushrooms, sliced
4	pepperoncini, sliced
2	ounces part-skim mozzarella, shredded

Preheat the grill. Coat a grill rack with cooking spray; place on the grill. Place the pizza crust on a round pizza pan with holes. Brush the oil over the crust. Spread the tomatoes, pepperoni, mushrooms and pepperoncini over the crust. Top with the mozzarella cheese.

Place on the grill rack. Grill over direct low heat until the cheese melts, about 10 minutes. Let cool for 3 minutes before slicing.

HELPFUL HINT

Unless you have a pizza peel (or a cookie sheet with only one side that you can use like a peel), it's easiest to cook the pizza on a pan.

PER SERVING:
Calories: 217
Fat (g): 8.2
Saturated Fat (g): 2
Cholesterol (mg): 14
Carbohydrates (g): 26.5
Sodium (mg): 587
Dietary Fiber (g): 0.3

QUICK PINTO BEAN BURRITOS

Inject no-fuss burritos with fast Tex-Mex character and flavor. And kick the heat out of the kitchen, to boot. How? Whip up these burritos and heat them on the grill. Perfect for rush-hour dining. Perfect for doubling or tripling for a crowd.

PREPARATION TIME:
15 minutes
COOKING TIME:
10 minutes
SERVINGS: 4

- 4 flour tortillas (10-inch)
- 1 cup nonfat sour cream
- ½ cup medium-hot salsa
- 2 tablespoons chopped cilantro
- ¾ cup shredded Monterey Jack cheese
- 2 small green sweet peppers, chopped
- 1 cup cooked pinto beans

Preheat the grill. Coat a grill rack with cooking spray; place on the grill.

Warm the tortillas in the microwave oven according to package directions to soften them. Spread the sour cream and salsa over the tortillas. Sprinkle with the cilantro. Place the Monterey Jack cheese, sweet peppers and pinto beans in the center. Fold up the ends and starting from one side, roll jelly-roll fashion. Wrap in foil and arrange on the grill. Grill until heated through, about 10 minutes.

HELPFUL HINT

Rinse and drain canned beans to remove excess sodium.

PER SERVING:
Calories: 338
Fat (g): 9.5
Saturated Fat (g): 4.2
Cholesterol (mg): 23
Carbohydrates (g): 46.9
Sodium (mg): 457
Dietary Fiber (g): 6

RED ONION AND PEPPER FOCACCIA

Ever feasted on focaccia (an Italian bread dish similar to pizza) made in a wood-burning oven? The flavor is extraordinary, isn't it? In this quick and easy version, the grill duplicates that wonderful smoky flavor. And a prepared crust takes away the hassle of making your own dough. Red onion and red sweet pepper play well with mozzarella cheese in the topping.

PREPARATION TIME:
15 minutes
COOKING TIME:
10 minutes
SERVINGS: *4*

1	prepared thin pizza crust (12-inch)
1	teaspoon olive oil
4	cloves garlic, chopped
1	dried cayenne, seeded and minced
1	red onion, thinly sliced
1	small red sweet pepper, cut into thin rings
2	ounces part-skim mozzarella cheese, shredded
8	basil leaves, minced (garnish)

Preheat the grill. Coat a grill rack with cooking spray; place on the grill. Place the crust on a round pizza pan (preferably one with holes). Brush the oil over the crust. Sprinkle the garlic and cayenne over the crust. Layer the onion, pepper and mozzarella cheese.

Place on the grill rack. Grill over direct low heat until the cheese melts, about 10 minutes. Garnish with the basil. Slice and serve immediately.

HELPFUL HINT

The focaccia can be cooked directly on the grill rack, but it's easiest to handle if you use a pan.

PER SERVING:
Calories: 385
Fat (g): 10.5
Saturated Fat (g): 1.6
Cholesterol (mg): 17
Carbohydrates (g): 57
Sodium (mg): 693
Dietary Fiber (g): 2.4

THYMELY CHICKEN IN PITA POCKETS

Whoever invented pita bread pockets was a genius. These nutty-tasting individual flat breads are naturals, as the Greeks know, for stuffing with flavor partners like minty thyme and tender chicken, cool cucumber and creamy yogurt. This whole production—from making the cucumber sauce to grilling the chicken—takes but 30 minutes, and it makes for a complete, light meal.

PREPARATION TIME:

10 minutes

COOKING TIME:

20 minutes

SERVINGS: *4*

2 teaspoons olive oil

1 tablespoon plus 1 teaspoon snipped fresh thyme leaves

2 teaspoons grated lemon peel

1/2 teaspoon freshly grated black pepper

3/4 pound skinless, boneless chicken breasts

1/2 cup plain nonfat yogurt

1/2 cucumber, peeled, seeded and diced

1 scallion, minced

4 wheat pita pocket breads, split

1 cup alfalfa sprouts

Preheat the grill. Coat a grill rack with cooking spray; place on the grill. Whisk the oil, 2 teaspoons thyme, 1 teaspoon lemon peel and 1/4 teaspoon pepper in a small bowl until well mixed. Rub the thyme mixture over the chicken breasts. Arrange the chicken on the grill rack.

Grill over indirect medium heat until lightly browned, cooked through and the juices run clear, about 20 minutes, turning once. Transfer to a platter; slice into very thin short strips.

Whisk the yogurt, remaining 2 teaspoons thyme, 1 teaspoon lemon peel and 1/4 teaspoon pepper in a small bowl until well blended. Stir in the cucumber and scallion.

Divide the chicken among the pita breads. Spoon in the cucumber mixture and stuff in the sprouts.

PER SERVING:
Calories: 356
Fat (g): 7.2
Saturated Fat (g): 1.5
Cholesterol (mg): 73
Carbohydrates (g): 39
Sodium (mg): 426
Dietary Fiber (g): 5.5

HELPFUL HINT

Don't split the pita pockets; instead, cut them in half to create natural pockets.

SWEET SAUSAGE SANDWICHES

Jazz up an always popular grilled item, sweet pork sausage, with freshly roasted vegetables—red sweet pepper strips and red onion rings, to be specific. Serve everything tucked into Portuguese rolls, as done in this recipe, for a surefire mealtime hit.

PREPARATION TIME:

5 minutes

COOKING TIME:

20 minutes

SERVINGS: **4**

4 links sweet pork sausage
I large red sweet pepper, cut into thin strips
I medium red onion, thinly sliced
4 Portuguese rolls, split
4 tablespoons sweet India relish
4 leaves Boston lettuce

Preheat the grill. Coat a grill rack with cooking spray; place on the grill. Coat a grill basket or topper with cooking spray. Arrange the sausage on the grill rack. Arrange the pepper and onion in the basket.

Grill the sausage and vegetables over indirect medium heat until the sausage is cooked through and browned and the vegetables are tender, 16 to 20 minutes, turning with tongs several times. Tuck into the rolls along with the India relish and Boston lettuce.

HELPFUL HINT

The sweet pepper and onion may be done before the sausage. If that's the case, transfer the vegetables to a bowl. Cover to keep them warm until the sausage is ready.

PER SERVING:
Calories: 307
Fat (g): 10.7
Saturated Fat (g): 3.4
Cholesterol (mg): 23
Carbohydrates (g): 42.5
Sodium (mg): 678
Dietary Fiber (g): 2.8

sweet sides and endings

Amaretto Peaches

Angel's Piña Colada Dessert

Banana Splits

Butterscotch Pound Cake

Cinnamon Apples

Mixed Fruit Compote

Quick and Easy Pear Crisp

AMARETTO PEACHES

Sometimes simple is best, as in this recipe where just a splash of amaretto brings out the sensual sweetness of grilled peaches. Toasted almonds add a welcome crunch.

PREPARATION TIME:
5 minutes
COOKING TIME:
8 minutes
SERVINGS: **4**

4 peaches, halved and peeled
1 teaspoon amaretto
1 tablespoon sliced almonds, toasted
  Nonfat whipped topping (garnish)

Preheat the grill. Coat a grill rack with cooking spray; place on the grill. Arrange the peaches on the grill rack, cut side down. Grill over indirect medium heat until hot, about 8 minutes, turning with tongs once. Transfer to a platter and brush or drizzle the amaretto over the cut sides of the hot peaches. Top with the toasted almonds. Garnish with the whipped topping and serve at once.

HELPFUL HINTS

To pit a peach, cut the fruit vertically all the way around. Then, gently twist the two halves until one half frees itself from the pit. Use the point of the paring knife to pop the pit from the second half.

To toast almonds, spread them in a small nonstick skillet. Warm over medium heat until golden, about 5 minutes, shaking the pan or stirring the almonds frequently.

PER SERVING:
Calories: 53
Fat (g): 1.2
Saturated Fat (g): 0.1
Cholesterol (mg): 0
Carbohydrates (g): 10.3
Sodium (mg): 0
Dietary Fiber (g): 2

ANGEL'S PIÑA COLADA DESSERT

Here's a treat to die for: toasted angel food cake that's topped with a devilish splash of rum. Readily available coconut and hot-off-the-grill pineapple complete the piña colada trio of flavors. Use either canned or fresh ripe pineapple.

PREPARATION TIME:
5 to 10 minutes
COOKING TIME:
5 minutes
SERVINGS: **4**

1	tablespoon rum
1	teaspoon sugar
8	pineapple slices
4	slices angel food cake
2	tablespoons flaked coconut
2	cups lemon sherbet
	Nonfat whipped topping (garnish)

Whisk the rum and sugar in a small bowl until blended well.

Preheat the grill. Coat a grill rack with cooking spray; place on the grill. Arrange the pineapple slices and angel food cake slices on the grill rack. Grill over indirect medium heat until the pineapple is hot and lightly browned and the cake toasted, about 5 minutes, turning with tongs once. Transfer to individual dessert plates.

Arrange the pineapple on the cake. Drizzle the rum mixture over the pineapple and sprinkle the coconut over the pineapple. Serve with the sherbet and garnish with the whipped topping.

HELPFUL HINT

If you've baked your own angle food cake, let it cool completely before slicing it. Use a serrated knife and a gentle sawing motion for best results.

PER SERVING:
Calories: 376
Fat (g): 2.8
Saturated Fat (g): 1.9
Cholesterol (mg): 7
Carbohydrates (g): 81
Sodium (mg): 142
Dietary Fiber (g): 1

BANANA SPLITS

Usually, banana splits are a cool idea. But here they've got a hot new twist. The bananas and all the fixings (except the ice cream and whipped topping, of course) are cooked on the grill.

PREPARATION TIME:

5 to 10 minutes

COOKING TIME:

10 minutes

SERVINGS: *4*

4	bananas, peeled, halved lengthwise
1/4	cup brown sugar
1	tablespoon plus 1 teaspoon walnut pieces
2	teaspoons crème de cacao
2	teaspoons whipped butter, cut into small pieces
2	cups vanilla fat-free ice cream
	Nonfat whipped topping (garnish)

Preheat the grill. Coat a grill rack with cooking spray; place on the grill.

Cut four 12 x 24-inch rectangles of foil. Place both halves of a banana in the center of each piece of foil. Cut into 2-inch slices. Sprinkle the brown sugar, walnuts and crème de cacao over the bananas. Dot with the butter. Bring up the edges of the foil and fold to seal. Arrange on the grill rack.

Grill over direct medium heat until the sugar has melted and the bananas are hot, about 6 minutes. Divide the ice cream among 4 dessert dishes and surround with the bananas. Pour the brown sugar mixture over the bananas and ice cream. Top with the whipped topping. Serve immediately.

HELPFUL HINT

Use pristine foil with no teeny, tiny holes or tears to wrap the bananas or the sweet crème de cacao topping will drip into the grill.

PER SERVING:
Calories: 370
Fat (g): 6.6
Saturated Fat (g): 1.5
Cholesterol (mg): 4
Carbohydrates (g): 68
Sodium (mg): 93
Dietary Fiber (g): 3.1

BUTTERSCOTCH POUND CAKE

Got a sweet tooth? Then you'll love this easy dessert of grilled pound cake that's topped with ice cream and butterscotch sauce. The contrast between crisp hot pound cake and smooth cool ice cream is superb.

PREPARATION TIME:

5 minutes

COOKING TIME:

4 minutes

SERVINGS: **4**

4   slices (1 inch thick) low-fat or fat-free pound cake
2   cups vanilla fat-free ice cream
$\frac{1}{2}$ cup fat-free butterscotch-flavored topping
    Nonfat whipped topping

Preheat the grill. Coat a grill rack with cooking spray; place on the grill. Arrange the cake slices on the grill rack. Grill over indirect medium heat until golden, about 2 minutes on each side, turning with a spatula once.

Transfer to dessert plates. Top with the ice cream, butterscotch topping and whipped topping. Serve immediately.

HELPFUL HINT

Low-fat (and fat-free) pound cake is high in moisture and sugar and has a soft, sticky texture. To keep it from sticking to the grill rack, start with a very clean rack and coat it liberally with cooking spray.

PER SERVING:
Calories: 282
Fat (g): 0.1
Saturated Fat (g): 0.1
Cholesterol (mg): 1
Carbohydrates (g): 67.7
Sodium (mg): 352
Dietary Fiber (g): 0.6

CINNAMON APPLES

Apples, brown sugar, cinnamon—a winning threesome that's at home with any chicken, turkey or pork roast. Enjoy these apples as a side dish, in a sandwich or as a dessert.

PREPARATION TIME:
5 minutes

COOKING TIME:
10 to 20 minutes

SERVINGS: **4**

- 2 tablespoons brown sugar
- 1 teaspoon cinnamon
- 1/2 cup water
- 1/4 cup lemon juice
- 2 Rome apples, cored and cut into 1/4-inch slices

Preheat the grill. Coat a grill rack with cooking spray; place on the grill. Combine the brown sugar and cinnamon in a small bowl, stirring until well mixed.

Whisk the water and lemon juice in a medium-size bowl. Dip the apple slices into the mixture. Arrange on the grill rack. Grill over indirect low heat just until hot and softened but not dry, 5 to 8 minutes on a side, turning with a spatula or tongs once. Transfer to a platter and sprinkle the cinnamon-sugar mixture over the apples.

HELPFUL HINT

Most any apple will work in this recipe; Rome, Golden Delicious and Cortland are especially nice.

PER SERVING:
Calories: 72
Fat (g): 0.3
Saturated Fat (g): 0
Cholesterol (mg): 0
Carbohydrates (g): 19
Sodium (mg): 4
Dietary Fiber (g): 2.2

MIXED FRUIT COMPOTE

So many luscious fruits take superbly to grilling that I kept adding and adding and adding to this lively recipe. Feel free to customize the mix, including or eliminating fruit according to availability. Next time, I'll also use apricots and grapefruit. . . or maybe grapes. . . or. . .

PREPARATION TIME:

20 minutes

COOKING TIME:

10 to 15 minutes

SERVINGS: **8**

2	plums, cut into bite-size pieces
1	nectarine, cut into bite-size pieces
1	pear, cut into bite-size pieces
1	apple, cut into bite-size pieces
1	banana, cut into bite-size pieces
1	orange, cut into bite-size pieces
2	pineapple slices, cut into bite-size pieces
2	kiwifruit, cut into bite-size pieces
2	cups white grape juice
$\frac{1}{2}$	cup raisins
1	stick cinnamon
1	whole clove
$\frac{1}{8}$	teaspoon nutmeg
	Mint leaves (garnish)
	Lemon wedges (garnish)

PER SERVING:
Calories: 288
Fat (g): 1.1
Saturated Fat (g): 0.2
Cholesterol (mg): 0
Carbohydrates (g): 73
Sodium (mg): 8
Dietary Fiber (g): 7.4

Preheat the grill and place a grill rack on the grill. Coat a grill wok, basket or topper with cooking spray; place on the grill. Spread the plums, nectarine, pear, apple, banana, orange, pineapple and kiwifruit over the bottom of the wok. Grill over indirect medium heat until the fruit is hot and begins to soften, 10 to 15 minutes, stirring gently once or twice.

Transfer to a large bowl and immediately pour in the grape juice. Stir in the raisins, cinnamon, clove and nutmeg. Let steep for 1 hour; discard the cinnamon and clove. Serve garnished with mint and lemon wedges.

HELPFUL HINT

For the most part, fruit peel adds nice texture and color to this dish. Peel only the pineapple, orange, banana and kiwifruit.

QUICK AND EASY PEAR CRISP

Traditionally fruit crisps are baked to sweet perfection. In this simple rendition, the pears cook on the grill while the oat and almond topping toasts on the stove top.

1/2	teaspoon cinnamon
2	tablespoons quick oats
2	tablespoons sliced almonds
4	Bartlett pears, peeled, halved and cored
2	teaspoons whipped butter
2	tablespoons brown sugar
	Nonfat whipped topping (garnish)

PREPARATION TIME:
5 to 10 minutes
COOKING TIME:
5 to 10 minutes
SERVINGS: **4**

Preheat the grill. Coat a grill rack with cooking spray; place on the grill.

Combine the cinnamon, oats and almonds in a small nonstick skillet, stirring to mix well. Toast the mixture over medium heat until the oats and almonds are lightly browned and fragrant, 5 to 10 minutes, stirring often.

Arrange the pears on the grill rack. Grill over indirect medium heat until lightly browned, about 10 minutes, turning with tongs once. Transfer to dessert plates.

Dot the cut sides with the butter. Sprinkle the oats mixture and brown sugar over the top. Garnish with the whipped topping.

HELPFUL HINT

The skin on pears toughens *slightly* as the fruit cooks. In this recipe, whether to peel or not is really up to you.

PER SERVING:
Calories: 337
Fat (g): 7
Saturated Fat (g): 1.7
Cholesterol (mg): 5
Carbohydrates (g): 63.7
Sodium (mg): 54
Dietary Fiber (g): 8.9

marina
sauce

des, mops,
s and rubs

Basic Barbecue Sauce

Lime-Jalapeño Marinade

White Wine Marinade

Easy Paprika Mop

Lemon-Mustard Mop

Fragrant Herb Rub

Pecan Rub

Orange-Tarragon Glaze

Raspberry-Nutmeg Glaze

Pesto Paste

marinades, mops, sauces and rubs

BASIC BARBECUE SAUCE

Every home cook and famous chef has a favorite barbecue sauce. Here's mine—a mild tomato-based sauce that's a take-off on one my grandmother used to whip up.

2 cups tomato sauce

½ cup minced dried onions

2 teaspoons olive oil

¼ cup cider vinegar

1½ tablespoons light brown sugar

2 teaspoons prepared mustard

¼ teaspoon liquid hickory smoke (optional)

Combine the tomato sauce, onions, olive oil, cider vinegar, brown sugar, mustard and hickory smoke, if desired, in a medium-size saucepan, stirring to mix well. Simmer over medium-high heat for 5 minutes, stirring occasionally.

Serve hot over chicken, beef, ham or pork.

HELPFUL HINT

Store extra sauce, covered, in the refrigerator for up to 4 days. Reheat the sauce before using it.

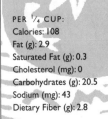

PREPARATION TIME:

5 minutes

COOKING TIME:

5 minutes

MAKES: *about 2¼ cups (enough for 2 to 3 pounds of chicken, beef, ham or pork)*

PER ¼ CUP:
Calories: 108
Fat (g): 2.9
Saturated Fat (g): 0.3
Cholesterol (mg): 0
Carbohydrates (g): 20.5
Sodium (mg): 43
Dietary Fiber (g): 2.8

LIME-JALAPEÑO MARINADE

Lime dominates in this simple marinade. Use it to give poultry, beef or pork the flavor essence of Caribbean cuisine.

PREPARATION TIME:

5 minutes

COOKING TIME:

10 minutes to use as a baste

MAKES: *about ¹/₂ cup (enough for 1 pound of chicken, turkey, beef or pork)*

Juice of 2 limes
¹/₄ cup dry white wine
¹/₄ teaspoon seeded, minced dried jalapeño
2 teaspoons olive oil
2 teaspoons lime peel
1 clove garlic, crushed

Combine the lime juice, wine, jalapeño, oil, lime peel and garlic in a small bowl, stirring until well mixed. Pour over poultry, beef or pork in a self-sealing plastic bag or a shallow bowl and marinate in the refrigerator for 30 minutes to 4 hours.

After marinating, simmer for 10 minutes before using to baste poultry, beef or pork as it grills. Discard excess marinade.

HELPFUL HINTS

Wear rubber gloves when seeding and mincing jalapeños. Capsaicin, the potent substance that gives chilies their delightful heat, can sting your fingertips. Wash the work surface before cutting other foods on it.

For safety reasons, always simmer a marinade that has come in contact with raw meat before using it as a baste. Discard excess.

PER 2 TABLESPOONS:
Calories: 40
Fat (g): 2.3
Saturated Fat (g): 0.3
Cholesterol (mg): 0
Carbohydrates (g): 3.4
Sodium (mg): 1.7
Dietary Fiber (g): 0.3

WHITE WINE MARINADE

Transform ordinary into extraordinary: Spoon these wine and thyme infused onions over beef steak or lamb chops during the last 10 minutes of grilling.

- ½ cup dry white wine
- 1 small onion, minced
- 3 cloves garlic, crushed
- ½ teaspoon freshly ground black pepper
- 2 teaspoons olive oil
- 1 tablespoon fresh thyme leaves or 1 teaspoon dried

Combine the white wine, onion, garlic, pepper, oil and thyme in a small bowl, stirring until well mixed. Pour over beef, lamb or pork in a self-sealing plastic bag or a shallow bowl and marinate in the refrigerator for 30 minutes to 8 hours.

After marinating, simmer for 10 minutes before using to baste beef, lamb or pork as it grills. Discard excess marinade.

HELPFUL HINT

This marinade can be made ahead and stored, covered, in the refrigerator for up to 2 days.

PREPARATION TIME:
5 minutes
COOKING TIME:
10 minutes to use as a baste
MAKES: *about ½ cup (enough for 1 pound of beef, lamb or pork)*

PER 2 TABLESPOONS:
Calories: 50
Fat (g): 2.3
Saturated Fat (g): 0.3
Cholesterol (mg): 0
Carbohydrates (g): 2.6
Sodium (mg): 2.6
Dietary Fiber (g): 0.5

EASY PAPRIKA MOP

Thick, slightly sweet and satisfying—this everyday-ketchup-and-mild-paprika sauce comes together in a split second (well, maybe more like a couple of minutes) and tastes great on chicken, beef or pork.

PREPARATION TIME:

5 minutes

COOKING TIME:

1 minute

MAKES: **about ³/₄ cup (enough for 1 pound of chicken, beef or pork)**

¹/₂ cup ketchup
2 tablespoons cider vinegar
2 tablespoons paprika
2 teaspoons Worcestershire sauce
2 teaspoons light or dark brown sugar

Whisk the ketchup, vinegar, paprika, Worcestershire sauce and brown sugar in a small saucepan until well blended. Simmer over medium heat for 1 minute; keep warm on the side of the grill. "Mop," or baste, chicken, beef or pork 2 or 3 times after turning.

HELPFUL HINTS

Always slather a warm "mop" over foods being grilled. Applying a cold one will chill the food and slow its cooking—and may even encourage the growth of unwanted bacteria.

When done, wash the mop (utensil) thoroughly to remove any bacteria it might have picked up from the food.

PER 2 TABLESPOONS:
Calories: 41
Fat (g): 0.4
Saturated Fat (g): 0.1
Cholesterol (mg): 0
Carbohydrates (g): 8.9
Sodium (mg): 227
Dietary Fiber (g): 0.7

LEMON-MUSTARD MOP

Lemon and mustard flavors fairly pop in this fast-to-whisk-up light mop. Enjoy it on poultry, fish, beef or pork.

Juice of 1 lemon
1/3 cup fat-free, reduced-sodium chicken broth
1 tablespoon minced dried onions
2 teaspoons olive oil
1 teaspoon Dijon mustard
1/2 teaspoon poultry seasoning
1/4 teaspoon garlic powder
2 teaspoons grated lemon peel

PREPARATION TIME:
5 minutes
COOKING TIME:
1 minute
MAKES: **about 1/2 cup (enough for 1 pound of chicken, beef, fish or pork)**

Whisk the lemon juice, chicken broth, onions, oil, mustard, poultry seasoning, garlic powder and lemon peel in a small saucepan until well combined. Simmer over medium heat for 1 minute; keep warm on the side of the grill. "Mop," or baste, chicken, beef, fish or pork 2 or 3 times after turning.

HELPFUL HINT

If you don't have Dijon mustard in stock, try a spicy brown variety.

PER 2 TABLESPOONS:
Calories: 34
Fat (g): 2.4
Saturated Fat (g): 0.3
Cholesterol (mg): 0
Carbohydrates (g): 2.9
Sodium (mg): 22
Dietary Fiber (g): 0.3

FRAGRANT HERB RUB

Orange and rosemary are the dominant flavors in this super-easy, dried-herb rub. It's perfect for perking up beef, pork, fish or poultry.

PREPARATION TIME:

5 minutes

COOKING TIME:

none

MAKES: **about 4 teaspoons (enough for 1 pound of chicken, turkey, fish, beef or pork)**

I   teaspoon dried thyme

I   teaspoon dried rosemary

I   teaspoon dried basil

I   teaspoon fresh or dried orange peel

Whisk the thyme, rosemary, basil and orange peel in a small bowl. Rub over poultry, fish, beef or pork.

HELPFUL HINT

This mixture can be prepared a few hours ahead. Store it in a covered container in a cool, dry place.

PER TEASPOON:
Calories: 3
Fat (g): 0.1
Saturated Fat (g): 0
Cholesterol (mg): 0
Carbohydrates (g): 0.7
Sodium (mg): 0.5
Dietary Fiber (g): 0.4

PECAN RUB

Here, ground pecans and whole mustard seeds form a flavor-studded crust for chicken breasts, turkey tenders or pork chops.

2 tablespoons pecan pieces, ground
1 tablespoon yellow mustard seeds
1 tablespoon brown sugar
1 teaspoon fresh or dried lemon peel
$\frac{1}{4}$ teaspoon freshly ground black pepper

Combine the pecans, mustard seeds, brown sugar, lemon peel, and pepper in a small bowl, stirring until well mixed. Rub over chicken, turkey or pork.

HELPFUL HINT

Moisture often causes fresh lemon peel to clump. So for a rub that's truly crumbly, use dried peel.

PREPARATION TIME:
5 minutes
COOKING TIME:
none
MAKES: **about $\frac{1}{4}$ cup (enough for 1 pound of chicken, turkey or pork)**

PER 1 TABLESPOON:
Calories: 47
Fat (g): 2.9
Saturated Fat (g): 0.2
Cholesterol (mg): 0
Carbohydrates (g): 5.1
Sodium (mg): 28
Dietary Fiber (g): 0.7

ORANGE-TARRAGON GLAZE

PREPARATION TIME:

5 minutes

COOKING TIME:

1 minute

MAKES: *about $1/2$ cup (enough for 1 pound of chicken, turkey or pork)*

So many glazes are super-sweet. But this one has a nice pungent hint—thanks to tarragon. To bring out dried tarragon's flavor, crush the leaves between your fingers before adding them to the glaze mix.

$1/2$ cup orange marmalade
1 teaspoon dried tarragon
1 teaspoon Dijon mustard

Combine the marmalade, tarragon and mustard in a small saucepan, stirring to mix well. Warm over medium-low heat until the marmalade is melted, about 1 minute, stirring constantly. Spread over the chicken, turkey or pork near the end of cooking.

HELPFUL HINT

Marmalades and preserves melt quickly, without constant stirring, in a microwave. Simply combine the ingredients in a small microwave-safe glass bowl and microwave on Medium for 30 to 40 seconds.

PER 2 TABLESPOONS:
Calories: 106
Fat (g): 0.2
Saturated Fat (g): 0
Cholesterol (mg): 0
Carbohydrates (g): 28.3
Sodium (mg): 13
Dietary Fiber (g): 2.1

RASPBERRY-NUTMEG GLAZE

Nutmeg enlivens this extra-simple glaze with a smidgen of sharp spice taste. If you don't have any raspberry vinegar, feel free to use white wine vinegar instead.

$1/2$ cup raspberry preserves
2 teaspoons raspberry vinegar
$1/4$ teaspoon nutmeg

Combine the raspberry preserves, raspberry vinegar and nutmeg in a small saucepan, stirring to mix well. Warm over medium-low heat until the preserves are melted, about 1 minute, stirring constantly. Spread over the chicken, turkey or pork near the end of cooking.

HELPFUL HINT

For maximum sensory impact, grate the nutmeg right before using it. The preground variety, while convenient, has much less flavor.

PREPARATION TIME:
5 minutes
COOKING TIME:
1 minute
MAKES: *about $1/2$ cup (enough for 1 pound of chicken, turkey or pork)*

PER 2 TABLESPOONS:
Calories: 110
Fat (g): 0.1
Saturated Fat (g): 0
Cholesterol (mg): 0
Carbohydrates (g): 28
Sodium (mg): 5
Dietary Fiber (g): 0.4

PESTO PASTE

This magnificent pesto—a light version of the classic basil sauce originating in Genoa, Italy—is delicious not only as a rub for poultry, beef and pork but as a spread for crostini. Enjoy!

PREPARATION TIME:

10 minutes

COOKING TIME:

1 minute

MAKES: *about ¼ cup (enough for 1 pound of chicken, turkey, beef or pork)*

1	tablespoon olive oil
2	teaspoons grated Parmesan cheese
½	cup chopped fresh basil
2	teaspoons toasted sunflower seeds

Combine the oil, Parmesan cheese, basil and sunflower seeds in the bowl of a mini food processor. Process at medium speed until the mixture forms a paste, 30 to 60 seconds, stopping and scraping the sides of the bowl as necessary. Spread over chicken, turkey, beef or pork before or after cooking.

HELPFUL HINT

To keep fresh basil perky for up to 5 days, place the stems in a container of cool water. Loosely cover the leaves and container with a plastic bag; secure the bottom of the bag with an elastic band. Refrigerate and change the water daily.

PER 1 TABLESPOON:
Calories: 31
Fat (g): 2.7
Saturated Fat (g): 0.7
Cholesterol (mg): 2
Carbohydrates (g): 0.6
Sodium (mg): 47
Dietary Fiber (g): 0.4

appendices

It's dinnertime. And time to grill up something that tickles your taste buds. But you don't want to use a specific recipe. Then follow these simple steps and check the convenient tables below for suggested grilling times: Preheat the grill and coat the grill rack with cooking spray. Place the rack on the grill, then arrange the food on the rack. Grill, turning meats once or vegetables several times until the food is cooked to the desired doneness.

Meat	Grilling Temperature	Doneness*	Grilling Time** (minutes)
Beef			
Round	Medium	Medium	20 to 40
Sirloin steak	Medium	Medium	20 to 30
T-bone	Medium	Medium	20 to 30
Patties	Medium	Cooked throughout	20 to 25
Ham			
Precooked slice	Medium	Hot throughout	10 to 20
Lamb			
Chop	Medium	Medium	15 to 25
Patties	Medium	Cooked throughout	20 to 30
Pork			
Tenderloin	Medium	Medium	30 to 35
Chop	Medium	Medium	20 to 25
Veal			
Chop	Medium	Medium	20 to 25
Kabobs			
Beef, lamb, pork	Medium	Medium	15 to 25

Sausage			
Precooked	Medium	Hot throughout; lightly browned	15 to 30
Uncooked	Medium	Cooked throughout; lightly browned	30 to 45

* Note: Cook to these minimum internal temperatures:
  • beef, lamb, veal—145°F
  • ground beef, lamb, veal—160°F
  • all pork—160°F
** Note: Indirect grilling for minimum flaring and charring.

Poultry	Grilling Temperature	Doneness*	Grilling Time** (minutes)
Chicken			
Skinless, boneless breast	Medium	Cooked throughout, juices clear	15 to 20
Bone-in breast	Medium	Cooked throughout, juices clear	20 to 30
Drumstick	Medium	Cooked throughout, juices clear	35 to 45
Thigh	Medium	Cooked throughout, juices clear	20 to 25
Turkey			
Skinless breast cutlets	Medium	Cooked throughout, juices clear	15 to 25
Skinless breast slices	Medium	Cooked throughout, juices clear	15 to 20

155

	Grilling Temperature	Doneness	Grilling Time (minutes)
Skinless breast tenderloin	Medium	Cooked throughout, juices clear	20 to 35
Patties	Medium	Cooked throughout, juices clear	20 to 30
Kabobs	Medium	Cooked throughout, juices clear	15 to 20
Sausage			
Precooked	Medium	Hot throughout; lightly browned	15 to 30
Uncooked	Medium	Cooked throughout; lightly browned	30 to 45

* Note: Cook to these minimum internal temperatures:
- poultry pieces—160°F
- ground poultry—165°F

** Note: Indirect grilling for minimum flaring and charring.

Seafood	Grilling Temperature	Doneness*	Grilling Time** (minutes)
Steak or fillet	Medium	Opaque and flakes; cooked throughout	5 per ½-inch thickness
Cubes	Medium	Opaque and flakes; cooked throughout	5 to 10
Sea Scallops	Medium	Opaque; cooked throughout	5 to 10
Shrimp	Medium	Opaque; cooked throughout	5 to 10

* Note: Cook to this minimum internal temperature:
- all fish—160°F

** Note: Indirect grilling for minimum flaring and charring.

Vegetable	Grilling Temperature	Doneness	Grilling Time* (minutes)
Asparagus	Medium	Tender	3 to 5
Baby carrots	Medium	Tender	3 to 5 (after precooking for 3 to 5 minutes)
Corn on the cob (wrapped in foil or damp husk)	Medium	Tender	10 to 20
Eggplant slices	Medium	Tender and lightly browned	15 to 30 (depending on thickness)
Fennel wedges	Medium	Tender	15 to 30
Potatoes	Medium	Tender	10 to 15 (after precooking for 10 to 15 minutes)
Onion slices	Medium	Tender; lightly browned	10 to 20 (depending on thickness)
Summer squash slices (yellow or zucchini)	Medium	Tender; lightly browned	5 to 10 (depending on thickness)
Summer squash quartered (yellow or zucchini)	Medium	Tender; lightly browned	5 to 15 (depending on size)
Sweet peppers	Medium	Tender; lightly browned	5 to 15 minutes
		Charred	10 to 20 minutes
Tomatoes, cherry or plum	Medium	Tender	3 to 10 minutes (depending on size)

* Note: Direct grilling; there is no fat to cause flaring and charring.

Fruit	Grilling Temperature	Doneness	Grilling Time* (minutes)
Apple slices	Medium	Tender; lightly browned	5 to 10
Nectarine halves	Medium	Tender; lightly browned	5 to 10
Peach halves	Medium	Tender; lightly browned	5 to 10
Pear halves	Medium	Tender; lightly browned	5 to 10
Pineapple slices	Medium	Tender; lightly browned	5 to 10

* Note: Direct grilling; there is no fat to cause flaring and charring.

Acorn squash: Thick-skinned and hard, this winter squash has mild-tasting, orange-colored flesh and a dark-green exterior. It's perfectly suited to baking and stuffing, and its seeds can be cleaned and roasted for snacking.

Albacore: This is the only tuna that can be called "white." Of all the tunas, it has the lightest meat and its flavor is the mildest. It's also the most expensive.

Alfalfa sprouts: Crisp, tender and delicate, these are germinated alfalfa seeds. They taste mildly nutty, and are tiny, white and green. They're best eaten raw. Look for them in the produce section of almost any large supermarket. At home, store them in their original packaging or in a plastic bag in the refrigerator for up to 2 days.

Almonds: These popular nuts come in shelled, unshelled, whole, sliced, slivered, chopped, blanched, raw, smoked, candied and paste form. Toasting intensifies their delightful flavor. Store unshelled almonds in an air-tight container in a cool, dry place for several months. Keep shelled nuts in the refrigerator for up to 6 months or in the freezer for up to 1 year.

Amaretto: An almond liqueur that's very smooth and sweet. It's usually served after dinner and often flavors rich-tasting desserts.

Artichoke hearts: The innermost, tender leaves of the green globe artichoke. Whole artichokes are available fresh; artichoke hearts and bottoms are available canned and may come marinated, packed in oil, or packed in water. The hearts also are available frozen.

Arugula: This a musky, peppery-tasting green that resembles radish leaves in appearance. Also known as rocket, it makes a lively addition to salads as well as soups. Purchase small, fresh-looking greens and use them within 2 days. Store, unwashed, in a plastic bag in the refrigerator.

Balsamic vinegar: Made from a very sweet grape and aged in wooden barrels for 10 years or more, balsamic vinegar tastes sweeter and more mellow than most other vinegars. It is dark brown in color, fairly pricey, and delightful in salads and marinades. Look for it in almost any large supermarket.

Baste: To spoon or brush a liquid over food as it cooks to flavor the food and keep it moist. Basting liquids include melted butter, pan drippings, broth, fruit juice, marinade, glaze or sauce.

Bean thread noodles: Also called *cellophane noodles, Chinese vermicelli, glass noodles* and *harusame*. Made from mung beans, these noodles are sold dried in cellophane packages and must be soaked in hot water for a few minutes before they're added to most dishes. Translucent at first, the noodles readily soak up the flavors and color of an accompanying sauce. Bean thread noodles are available in most supermarkets and in Asian groceries.

Belgian endive: Also known as *French endive, witloof chicory* and *witloof* (which means "white leaf" in French). This small, cone-shaped garden vegetable is just 5 to 6 inches long; its leaves are compact, creamy yellow and slightly bitter tasting. Eaten either raw or cooked. Look for tightly packed heads that are firm and blemish free. Store in a plastic bag in the refrigerator for up to 3 days.

Bell peppers: See **Peppers**.

Blacktip shark: A white, mild-tasting, firm-textured fish that adapts quite well to grilling.

Bleu cheese: A general term for any of the French blue- and green-veined cheeses, all of which are sharp tasting and usually crumbly. The American and English cheeses of similar types are spelled "blue" cheese.

Brochette: In French, brochette mean "skewer." *En brochette* refers to meat or vegetables cooked on a skewer.

Bruschetta: Simply put, this is garlic bread. In Italy, bruschetta is made by rubbing garlic over toasted bread slices, then drizzling olive oil over the bread. The slices are seasoned with salt and pepper and heated.

Burrito: A Mexican dish consisting of a large flour tortilla stuffed with seasoned meat, cheese, beans and other vegetables. Shredded lettuce, diced tomatoes, salsa and sour cream may accompany the burrito.

Butternut squash: A hard squash with smooth, orange-colored flesh and tender beige skin. Look for squash that's 8 to 12 inches long with a 4- to 5-inch diameter base. The color should be beige; a tinge of green indicates the squash isn't ripe. Store in a dark, cool place with good ventilation where it will keep for 1 week to 6 months.

Butterscotch: This is a simple cooked sauce made of butter and brown sugar.

Cajun seasoning: May also be labeled *Cajun spice seasoning*. This is a sassy blend of garlic, onion, chilies, black pepper, mustard and celery. Each brand of this seasoning has its own exclusive combination, so all taste a little different. Try several to find the one you like best.

Canadian bacon: This cured and smoked lean pork loin is closer to ham than to what we traditionally call bacon. Though it's more expensive than regular bacon, the Canadian style is leaner and generally fully cooked (but read the label to be sure), so it shrinks little during cooking.

Caper: The flower bud of a Mediterranean shrub, the caper has a prized sour and slightly bitter flavor. Its size ranges from tiny (a French nonpareil variety) to medium (a Spanish variety) to large (an Italian variety that's as big as the end of your pinkie). Once picked, the bud is sun-dried, then packed in salt or a vinegar-salt brine. To remove some of the salt, rinse capers in cold water before using them. The flower buds of nasturtium, buttercup, marigold and broom are sometimes used as inexpensive substitutes for capers. Add capers to dishes right before serving.

Catfish: Much of the catfish found in supermarkets today has been farm raised. The fish is mild, low in fat and firm and is ideal for baking, broiling or grilling.

Chili powder: A spicy blend of six dried and ground seasonings: chili peppers, oregano, cumin, garlic, coriander and cloves. Chili powder provides the intense, characteristic flavors found in chilis and other popular Mexican- and Tex-Mex-style dishes. It's available in the spice aisle of most supermarkets.

Chili sauce: Thick and tangy, chili sauce makes for a delightful condiment or recipe ingredient. Basic to all chili sauces are tomatoes, sweet peppers, chili peppers, onions, celery, and spices. Most supermarkets carry chili sauce.

Chinese cabbage: Though there are many varieties of Chinese cabbage, the two most commonly available in the U.S. are bok choy and napa cabbage.

Bok choy: Also known as *pak-choi,* this cabbage variety has long, white celerylike stalks with large, deep green leaves. Its flavor is mild and it can be eaten raw or cooked. Select firm cabbages with crisp, bright green leaves. Store in plastic bags in the refrigerator for several days.

Napa cabbage: Also known as *nappa cabbage, Chinese cabbage, celery cabbage* and *Tientsin cabbage*. This non-heading cabbage has elongated, tightly curled leaves with large, white ribs. Its flavor is sweet and texture crisp. Select cabbages with tight, crisp bright leaves. Store in plastic bags in the refrigerator for several days.

Chinese chili sauce: A spicy condiment of chili peppers, garlic and vinegar. Look for it in jars in large supermarkets or Asian specialty groceries.

Chinese five-spice powder: True to its name, this seasoning (aka *five-spice powder*) has just five spices usually in equal parts: cinnamon, cloves, fennel seed, star anise and szechuan peppers. Look for it in the spice aisle of your supermarket, and use it to flavor up Asian-style stir-fries and other dishes.

Chinese wheat noodles: These fast-cooking, extremely thin noodles are made from wheat, water, salt and, occasionally, eggs. Their flavor is delicate and nutty. Look for them in your supermarket's ethnic aisle. If you can't find them, substitute extra-thin spaghetti or angel-hair pasta.

Chive: A close cousin to the onion, the chive has long, green, tubular leaves. Fresh, frozen and freeze-dried chives are available in most supermarkets. Use the various forms interchangeably in most recipes.

Cider vinegar: A mild, fruity vinegar made with fermented apple juice. Use it to add zing to vinaigrettes, marinades, bastes, sauces and mops.

Cilantro: Also called *Chinese parsley, Mexican parsley* and *fresh coriander*. Cilantro refers to the bright green, delicate-looking leaves of the coriander plant. Its scent is often described as musty, and its flavor is distinctive and entirely different from that of coriander seeds, which also come from the coriander plant. When buying this herb, a seasoning used extensively in Mexican, Caribbean and Asian cooking, look for bunches of perky green leaves. Store cilantro for up to a week in the refrigerator in a plastic bag. Wash the leaves just before using them.

Couscous: A quick-cooking pasta—it takes just 5 minutes to prepare—couscous is a staple in numerous North African cuisines. Look for this tasty alternative to rice in your supermarket's ethnic aisle. Couscous is also the name of a delicious entrée in which cracked wheat is steamed over a simmering stew of chicken, raisins, chick peas and spices in a special pot called a *couscoussière*.

Crème de cacao: A chocolate-flavored liqueur that's usually served after dinner and used in making desserts.

Cubanel pepper: See **Peppers.**

Cumin: A small, amber-colored seed resembling a miniature caraway seed, cumin is a parsley cousin. It has an aromatic, pungent, almost nutty flavor that dominates many Indian and Mexican dishes. Though most supermarkets carry both whole and ground cumin, get the whole seeds and grind your own if you want maximum fresh flavor.

Curry powder: Not a single spice, but a blend of up to 20 spices and herbs, including cumin, coriander, red pepper, fenugreek, cinnamon, allspice, fennel, ginger, black pepper, mace, nutmeg, cloves, poppy seeds, sesame seeds and turmeric. It's the turmeric that gives the blend its characteristic yellow color. For best flavor and to eliminate a raw taste, lightly toast curry powder in a small nonstick skillet before using it.

Dijon mustard: Originating in France, this is a popular grayish brown mustard made with brown or black mustard seeds, white wine and a blend of spices. It has a clean, sharp taste that complements many foods and dishes.

Ditalini: A short ($\frac{1}{4}$- to $\frac{1}{2}$-inch), wide hollow-tube pasta. It's sometimes called *thimbles* and is most often used in soups.

Dredge: To coat a food, such as pieces of chicken, with a dry ingredient, such as flour or cornmeal. Dredging can add flavor and help browning.

Duck sauce: Often called *plum sauce* and frequently served with Asian dishes of duck, pork or chicken, duck sauce is a thick, sweet-sour condiment made with plums, apricots, sugar and seasonings. It's widely available in supermarkets.

Fennel: Often mislabeled as *sweet anise*, fennel has a broad bulbous base, overlapping pale green stems and feathery greenery. Its flavor is mild anise- or licorice-like. Choose firm bulbs with crisp stems and bright, fresh-looking greenery. Store in a plastic bag in the refrigerator for up to 4 days.

Feta cheese: A white, crumbly cheese with a tangy flavor, feta is a classic Greek cheese made from sheep's, goat's or cow's milk. It's cured and stored in a salty brine and makes a zesty addition to salads and other dishes.

Focaccia: An Italian yeast bread similar to pizza. The bread is usually brushed with olive oil, then topped with thinly sliced vegetables, such as olives, onions and tomatoes.

Fontina: A creamy yet semifirm cow's milk cheese with a mild, nutty flavor. The cheese melts easily and is imported from Italy, Denmark and France. It's also made in the U.S.

Gingerroot: This is the gnarled, knobby root of a tropical and subtropical plant. Its aroma is pungent and spicy; its flavor, sweet and peppery. A signature seasoning in many Asian and East Indian dishes, gingerroot has a thin, tan skin, which should be removed before using, and pale yellowish flesh. Look for this flavorful root in your supermarket's produce section, and choose one with a smooth skin; wrinkling indicates a dry oldster. Gingerroot will keep on your counter for several days. Or peel it, cut it into 1-inch chunks and freeze it in a self-sealing plastic bag for up to 6 months. A 1-inch piece equals about 1 tablespoon when minced. The powdered, dried version has a markedly different flavor and is most often used in baked goods, such as gingersnaps.

Gorgonzola cheese: This is Italy's version of bleu cheese. A crumbly, white cheese that's streaked with bluish-green veins, it's made with cow's milk and is rich and creamy with a pungent, savory flavor.

Gouda: A mellow whole-milk, cow's milk cheese named for its city of origin: Gouda, Netherlands. The cheese is interchangeable with Edam, another whole-milk cheese from the Netherlands.

Guava: A sweet tropical fruit, guava ranges in size from one to four inches in diameter (most are about the size of an apple, two inches), has a yellow to green skin and pale yellow to bright red flesh. Choose guavas with good color and that give to gentle palm pressure. Ripen guavas at room temperature, then store in the refrigerator for up to 4 days.

Gyro: This is a popular Greek sandwich made with grilled lamb, onions, sweet peppers and a cucumber-yogurt sauce. The filling is wrapped in pita pocket bread.

Herbes de Provence: A traditional blend of six dried herbs—rosemary, marjoram, thyme, sage, anise seed and savory—that's typical of the cuisine of southern France. Use it to season chicken, pork, veal, fish and shrimp.

Herbs: See **Appendix Seven** for combinations.

Hickory smoke flavoring: See **Smoke flavoring**.

Hoisin sauce: This thick, reddish-brown, sweet-spicy condiment of soybeans, chili peppers, garlic, sugar, vinegar and spices is widely used in the cooking of southern China. In the U.S., it's available in Asian specialty markets as well as most supermarkets. After opening hoisin sauce, store it, tightly covered, in a glass jar in the refrigerator, where it will keep for a number of months.

Horseradish: Eye-watering hot—especially when fresh—horseradish is the root of a perennial plant that's grated for boosting the flavor of soups, sauces and spreads. The term also refers to a nippy condiment made of grated horseradish, white vinegar and seasonings. Both the root and the condiment, which is packed in jars, are available in supermarkets. Plan to use them quickly as they lose their potency with age.

Hot-pepper sauce: One of numerous Louisiana-style sauces made with hot chili peppers, vinegar and salt. The flavor and heat vary from brand to brand, some being relatively mild; others, are so scorching that a single drop fires up an entire dish or sauce. When using a hot sauce for the first time, cautiously add it to dishes, tasting the results after each drop.

Italian herb seasoning: This is a delightful herb blend of basil, oregano and thyme; occasionally garlic powder, red pepper and rosemary are included. Use the mix to give entrées and side dishes characteristic Italian flavor.

Italian sausage: A coarse pork sausage that's usually flavored with garlic and fennel seed or anise seed. It's available in two styles: hot (seasoned with red hot peppers) and sweet (without the peppers). If you're watching your fat intake, try one of the newer turkey versions. Available in most supermarkets.

Jalapeño pepper: See **Peppers**.

Jarlsberg: A Norwegian, partially skimmed cow's milk cheese with a taste similar to Swiss. It's one of the largest-selling imported cheeses in the U.S.

Jerk seasoning: Often called *Jamaican jerk seasoning,* this is a dry blend of chilies, thyme, cinnamon, ginger, allspice, cloves, garlic and onions. Originating in Jamaica, the blend is usually rubbed on meats, especially pork, or poultry for grilling. Small jars of jerk seasoning are available in supermarkets.

Kielbasa: Also labeled *kielbasy,* this is a robust, smoked Polish sausage that's mostly available precooked, but for best flavor, it's served hot. Traditional kielbasa contains pork and spices, but beef may be added. Newer turkey versions have less fat.

Kiwifruit: This small, sweet, juicy fruit has beautiful emerald-green flesh with tiny black seeds that form a decorative circle around a yellowish core. The edible skin is soft, fuzzy and brown; most people prefer to remove it. When ripe, kiwifruit will yield to light finger pressure. Select unblemished fruit but don't worry about it being underripe. Ripen kiwi at room temperature; placing it in a paper bag with an apple or banana will speed things along. Unripe kiwi will keep for 2 to 3 weeks; store ripe fruit in the refrigerator for 2 to 4 days.

Lemon pepper: A seasoning blend of grated lemon peel, or zest, and black pepper. Read the label before buying this blend; some brands contain more salt than pepper or lemon.

Lime: Closely resembling its cousin the lemon, the lime has a thin, green skin and juicy, pale green pulp. The variety of lime seen most often throughout the U.S. is the Persian lime. The Key lime (also sometimes called the *Mexican lime*), from which the famous Key lime pie gets its name, is grown in Florida but is usually found only in specialty produce markets. Look for brightly colored limes that are firm, plump and heavy for their size. The skin should be a deep green, smooth and slightly glossy. Yellowish skin indicates the lime is an oldie, but brownish spots generally don't affect flavor. Store limes in a plastic bag in the refrigerator for up to 10 days. Cut limes will keep the same way for up to 5 days. Bottled lime juice and frozen juice are available in many supermarkets.

Madeira: A fortified wine that's named after the Portuguese island, Madeira. Its color runs from pale golden to rich tawny, and its flavor can be anywhere from quite dry to very sweet. Just a small amount can bring lots of flavor to a dish.

Mafalda: Resembling tiny lasagna, mafalda, a pasta, is about 1 inch wide and has rippled edges. It's available in almost any supermarket with a large selection of dried pasta.

Maple syrup: This is the boiled and concentrated sap of the maple tree. In the U.S., the syrup comes in four grades: Grade AA (Fancy) is the most refined and has a mild flavor and light, delicate color; Grades A and B are a little less refined; Grade C is the least refined and has a very dark color and a robust, almost molasseslike flavor. Maple-flavored syrup and pancake syrup contain mostly corn syrup and little or no real maple (and they cost far less than the real thing!). Store opened maple syrup in the refrigerator.

Marinade: A seasoned liquid that flavors and tenderizes meats, poultry, fish or vegetables. Ingredients in marinades include an acid, spices and sometimes oil. A dry mixture or paste of herbs and spices that is rubbed onto food before cooking is occasionally referred to as a marinade. See **Marinate.**

Marinate: To allow meats, poultry, fish or vegetables to soak in a seasoned liquid to impart flavor and tenderize. Because most marinades contain an acid—vinegar, citrus juice, wine—marinating should be done in a stainless steel, glass or ceramic bowl or sturdy plastic bag. Never use aluminum; it'll react with the acid—to be specific, pit the container and add an off-flavor to the food. And always cover and refrigerate the food if marinating for longer than 15 minutes.

Marjoram: This delightful herb, a member of the mint family, is also called *sweet marjoram*. It has long, oval, gray-green leaves and a very mild oregano-like flavor. To retain its delicate taste, add marjoram to dishes toward the end of cooking.

Marsala: Imported from Sicily, this is a fortified wine with an intriguing smoky flavor that ranges from sweet to dry. Use sparingly to add delectable flavor to sauces, mops, bastes, marinades, gravies.

Mesclun: This is simply a potpourri of young salad greens such as arugula, dandelion, frisée, oak leaf, mâche, radicchio and sorrel. Select mesclun with crisp-looking leaves. Store in a plastic bag for up to 5 days. Rinse and blot dry just before using.

Mesquite flavoring: See **Smoke flavoring**.

Mint: A delightful herb with a cool, refreshing aftertaste. It comes in fresh and dried forms as well as extracts. The two most popular mints are spearmint and peppermint. Of the two, spearmint is the mildest. Choose mint with fresh-looking, even-colored leaves. To store, place the bunch, stems down, in a small glass of water, and cover the glass and leaves with a plastic bag. Refrigerate the whole thing, changing the water every few days. Stored this way, the mint should stay fresh for up to a week.

Molasses: Rich and quite sweet, molasses is a syrupy byproduct of sugarcane refining. Two types are generally available in supermarkets: light, which has a fairly mild flavor and may be used as a table syrup, and dark, which has a more distinct, robust flavor and is great for baking (gingersnap cookies, for example) and cooking (baked beans, for example).

Mops: Bastes and mops are essentially the same, mops being the preferred term in some barbecue circles. These flavorful sauces are applied to roasting meats with a cotton string device that resembles a miniature mop. For food safety, keep the mop warm while applying it to cooking meats and thoroughly wash the mopping device after cooking is complete. Today, some cooks prefer to use a spray bottle for applying the mop.

Mushrooms: Not a single food, but an intriguing family of wild and cultivated edible fungi that range in texture from delicate to meaty and in flavor from mild to nutty. Colors include white, golden and brown. When buying mushrooms, select those that are plump, firm and fresh looking. To clean them, wipe them with a damp towel or gently rinse them in cool water. Never soak fresh mushrooms; too much water dilutes and ruins their flavor. These are three popular and readily available varieties:

> **Common, or Button:** White in color (occasionally brown), these mild-flavored, small mushrooms range in size from $1/2$ inch to 3 inches in diameter. Look for their familiar umbrella shape.

> **Portobello:** These huge brown mushrooms—caps often measure as much as 6 inches across—are the mature relatives of the common, cultivated variety. Their texture is meaty and flavor, earthy. Creative ways to use these spectacular fungi: grilled whole caps in sandwiches; marinated, grilled whole caps as side dishes; thickly sliced and sautéed in salads and entrées; chopped and sautéed in soups and stews.

> **Shiitake:** Brown in color (occasionally with tan striations), a shiitake mushroom has these characteristics: a large floppy cap that's anywhere from 2 to 10 inches across; a tough, slender stem that's usually discarded; and a full-bodied flavor that some connoisseurs say is steaklike. Once available only in Asian groceries, shiitake mushrooms can now be found in most large supermarkets but tend to be pricey.

Mustard seeds: These are the seeds of mustard plants, the peppery greens belonging to the same family as broccoli, brussels sprouts, kale, collards and kohlrabi. The seeds themselves come in three colors: black, brown and yellow,

yellow being the most common and most readily available. Use whole, cracked or ground.

Nachos: Crisp tortilla chips topped with cheese and chilies and served as a snack or appetizer.

Nutmeg: A hard, brownish seed with a warm, spicy-sweet flavor, nutmeg is sold ground and whole. Expect to get the best flavor from freshly ground nutmeg.

Paprika: A special variety of red sweet pepper that has been dried and ground for use as a seasoning and garnish. Though several areas of the world—notably Spain, California, South America and Hungary—produce paprika, the Hungarian variety is considered by many gourmands to be the standout. Paprika loses its flavor and color fairly quickly; store it in the refrigerator to extend its life.

Peel: The outer skin, or rind, of fruit or vegetables. When grating citrus peel, go no deeper than the colored part. The white area, or pith, tends to be bitter. Citrus peel is also called *zest*.

Pepperoncini: Also known as *Tuscan peppers*. These peppers have a sweet to medium-hot flavor and are most often sold pickled in jars.

Pepperoni: This is a highly seasoned beef and pork sausage that's often used on pizza in the U.S. Hailing from Italy, the sausage is firm, air-dried, and ready to eat. Sliced thinly or chopped coarsely and used in small quantities, it makes a delightful addition to many cooked dishes.

Peppers, sweet and hot: Crisp, colorful, flavorful, mild, hot, versatile, high in vitamin C, a good source of vitamin A, readily available—such attributes make peppers a favored vegetable in many cuisines: Chinese, Hungarian, Mexican, Thai, to name a few. Though there are tons of pepper varieties, all can be divided into two basic categories—sweet and hot. Here's a quick rundown of several popular and easily obtained varieties:

> **Anaheim:** A long, slender, moderately hot pepper (chili) that's also known as *New Mexican, long green, long red,* or *California.* They're the pepper of choice in the classic Mexican dish, chiles rellenos.

Ancho: A dried poblano chili that's 3 to 4 inches long, has a reddish-brown color and a mild to pungent flavor. The name means "wide chili" in Spanish.

Bell: A sweet, bell-shaped pepper that ranges in size from medium to very large and comes in several colors: green, red, yellow, orange, brown and purple. These peppers, often called *sweet peppers,* are suitable for roasting, stuffing, slicing, dicing and pureeing. Use them to add crunch, color and flavor in just about any chili, casserole or stew.

Cayenne: A long, thin, sharply pointed hot pepper that's either straight or curled. Generally, cayennes are sold when fully ripe and red in color. They're also available dried and ground into a powder.

Cubanel: A long (about 4 inches from tip to core), tapered pepper that's also known as an *Italian frying pepper* (and often spelled *cubanelle*). The peppers come in light green or yellow and are perfectly suited to sautéing.

Habanero: An extremely hot, small, orange-yellow chili. In Jamaica, it's known as *Scotch bonnet.* Because these peppers have so much firepower (200,000–300,000 Scoville Units, a relative heat measurement), you'll want to use them sparingly.

Jalapeño: A tapered, 2-inch-long, very hot pepper that's usually sold at the green, but mature, stage. These peppers are used to season cheese, jellies and sausage and are the most widely consumed chili in the United States.

Pimiento: A large, red, heart-shaped mild pepper that's usually sold in jars. Thick and meaty, pimientos (sometimes spelled *pimentos*) are ideal for roasting, if you can find them fresh.

Poblano: A very dark green, moderately hot pepper that resembles a stubby bell pepper with a tapered blossom end.

Serrano: A long, slender, very hot pepper that is usually sold green and often used in fresh salsas.

Picante sauce: A tomato-based condiment that has a smoother texture than salsa but has a similar flavor. Spiciness ranges from mild to mouth-searing.

Pickling spice: This is a pungent, dried spice-and-herb blend used for making pickles, relishes and other dishes. The mix varies according to manufacturer, but most include these basics: whole and broken allspice, bay leaves, cardamom, cinnamon, cloves, coriander, ginger, mace, mustard seeds and peppercorns. Look for the blend in almost any supermarket; it's is sold in small sealed bags, boxes or jars.

Pimiento: See **Peppers.**

Pita bread pocket: Often labeled simply as *pocket bread* or *pita,* this is a Middle Eastern white or whole wheat flat bread. When halved, the small, round bread forms two pockets that can be stuffed with all manner of goodies. These delightful breads can be found packaged in most supermarkets.

Poblano pepper: See **Peppers.**

Pork tenderloin: This is an extremely lean pork loin roast cut from the hog's back. When cooked, the meat is tender and white with clear juices. Tasty ways with this cut include roasting, stir-frying, sautéing and grilling as well as stewing.

Port: A sweet fortified wine that gets its name from the Portuguese city of Oporto. Tawny port, which is a brown color, is aged in wooden casks for 5–6 years while ruby port, which retains its red color, is aged for 3–4 years. Most often, these wines are served after a meal.

Portobello: See **Mushrooms.**

Potatoes: Several potato varieties grill quite nicely. Below are 3 that are especially pleasing. Select potatoes, no matter which variety, with clean, smooth skins, a firm texture and good shape. Store in a well-ventilated, dark place and avoid exposing them to light.

> **Red:** These thin-skinned potatoes have a firm and waxy texture that makes them ideal for potato salad.
>
> **Russet:** These are thick-skinned with a dry, mealy texture.
>
> **Yukon-Gold:** These are one of several varieties of thin-skinned potatoes with a buttery yellow flesh. Their flavor is mildly buttery as well.

Poultry seasoning: A dried and ground blend of 6 herbs and spices: thyme, sage, marjoram, rosemary, black pepper and nutmeg. Available in jars in supermarkets.

Pound cake: Originally this tender, rich cake was made with a pound each of butter, eggs, flour and sugar. Today's recipes are lighter; there's even a nonfat version.

Raspberry vinegar: A popular vinegar made from crushed raspberries and white vinegar. Available in gourmet groceries and some supermarkets.

Rice wine vinegar: This mild and slightly sweet vinegar is made from fermented rice and is widely used in Chinese and Japanese cooking. The vinegar is available in seasoned and unseasoned versions.

Romano cheese: A light yellow cheese with a nippy flavor and hard texture similar to that of Parmesan cheese. The two cheeses are generally grated, often added to Italian-style dishes and may be interchanged in recipes. For maximum flavor, use freshly grated cheese.

Rosemary: Cooks often describe the taste of this aromatic herb as piny. That's not surprising since its narrow green leaves resemble pine needles. Before using the leaves, chop the fresh variety and crush the dried form in a mortar and pestle or between your fingers. Rosemary is fairly assertive, especially when fresh, so apply it with restraint.

Sage: Sporting grayish-green leaves, which have a soft velvetlike surface, sage is an herb native to the Mediterranean. Its flavor stands out, pleasantly so, in traditional sausage mixes as well as poultry stuffings. When buying fresh sage, look for bunches of leaves with no blemishes or wilting. Keep sage, unwashed, in a plastic bag in the refrigerator for up to 4 days. Dried sage comes whole, rubbed (crumbled) and ground. Feel free to interchange rubbed and ground varieties in recipes. And because dried sage loses its spunk within 3 months, get it in small quantities.

Salsa verde: *Salsa* is the Mexican word for "sauce"; *verde*, the word for "green." Salsa verde is made from tomatillos, green chilies and cilantro. In the U.S., the most readily available salsa verde is in jars and has a chunky texture and mild flavor.

Sauerkraut: This a German condiment or side dish of brined (or pickled) shredded cabbage. It can be served warm or cold and is sold in supermarkets in cans and jars as well as fresh in plastic bags. To reduce the salt content, rinse and drain sauerkraut before using it.

Sea bass: A general term used to describe several saltwater fish. Black sea bass and striped bass are true members of the bass family. But fish labeled simply "sea bass" usually are members of the drum family. The fish is white, firm and moderately lean and suitable for baking, broiling and grilling.

Sesame oil: Pressed from sesame seeds, sesame oil comes in two versions: light and dark. Of the two, the light oil has a milder flavor and lighter color; use it to enhance salad dressings and for sautéing. Generally speaking, the darker version, with its intense flavor and color, is best for accenting Asian dishes; use it a drop or 2 at a time. Available in supermarkets and Asian specialty groceries.

Sesame seed: The tiny, flat, ivory-colored seed of a tropical herb plant. The seeds have a mild, nutty taste and a high oil content. Available in jars, sesame seeds can be stored in an air-tight container in the refrigerator for up to 6 months or in the freezer for up to 1 year. Stored at room temperature, they'll keep for about 3 months.

Shallot: Though related to onions, shallots resemble giant, brown garlic bulbs. Each bulb is composed of multiple cloves, each covered with a thin, papery skin. Select shallots that are plump and firm with no signs of wilting, sprouting or mold. And keep them in a cool, dry spot for up to a month. Prepare and use shallots, which are mild in flavor, in the same manner as onions.

Sherry: A fortified wine originating in Spain, sherry can range from dry and light to sweet and full-flavored. For best results, use a quality sherry, not a "cooking sherry," to punch up the flavor of sauces and bastes.

Smoke flavoring: Available in liquid form, smoke flavoring is nothing more than smoke concentrate in a water base. Popular flavors include hickory and mesquite. Use it to add a new dimension to sauces, bastes and marinades.

Sofrito: Spanish and Caribbean recipes are often flavored with this thick sauce. Traditionally, it's made of annatto seeds, pork (or rendered pork fat), onions, sweet peppers, garlic and herbs. Look for sofrito in jars in large supermarkets. Just a tablespoon or two will pump up marinades, mops, bastes and sauces.

Sorrel: A bitter salad green, or herb. Since it's assertive, use it sparingly in soups and salads. Look for crisp, bright leaves. Store in a plastic bag in the refrigerator for up to 4 days.

Spices: See **Appendix Seven** for combinations.

Stir-fry: To cook bite-size pieces of food quickly in a small amount of oil over high heat while stirring constantly and briskly. Also a dish that has been prepared by stir-frying.

Sun-dried tomatoes: As the name implies, these are tomatoes that have been dried, either in the sun or by another means. The resulting product is chewy, dark red, intensely flavored and slightly sweet. Sun-dried tomatoes come packed in oil in jars or dry-packed in cellophane packages. Soak the dry-packed version before adding them to soups, salads, sauces.

Sunflower seeds: Without the shells, these seeds are sometimes referred to as *sunflower kernels* or *sunflower nuts*. Store shelled and unshelled sunflower seeds in a tightly covered container in the refrigerator or freezer. Unshelled, raw kernels will keep for up to 1 year; roasted kernels will keep for up to 4 months. Salted versions are popular for snacking.

Szechuan sauce: A spicy Chinese condiment of miso, broad beans, rice wine vinegar, soy beans and red peppers. Available in jars in large supermarkets.

Tarragon: This herb, which has a distinctive almost licorice-like taste, is popular in French cooking and goes extremely well with orange. Tarragon's slender, pointed, dark green leaves flavor such foods as chicken and Béarnaise sauce. Use it with a little caution; its assertiveness can easily overwhelm other flavors. Dried tarragon is most readily available.

Teriyaki: A delightful homemade or commercially prepared sauce made of soy sauce, sake (or sherry), sugar, ginger and garlic. Popular uses for teriyaki, which has a Japanese origin, include marinating beef, poultry and seafood for broiling, grilling or stir-frying. The term "teriyaki" also refers to any dish made with a teriyaki sauce.

Thai seasoning: This is an exotic blend of spices—chili peppers, ginger, coriander, cumin, cinnamon, star anise, garlic, lemon peel and dried shallots—and may be labeled *Thai spice*. It imparts robust, warm flavor to noodles, rice, stews and other dishes. Thai spice can be found in the spice aisle of most supermarkets.

Thyme: A moderately assertive herb with tiny, dark green leaves, thyme plays well with basil and oregano and is often used in dishes with French or Italian accents. Slightly less assertive is lemon thyme, which has a delicate lemon fragrance. Thyme can be purchased fresh, dried and ground. Store thyme bunches in a plastic bag in the refrigerator for up to 5 days.

Tilapia: A variety of perch, tilapia is a white, mild and fine-textured fish. Also called *St. Peter's fish* and *Hawaiian sun fish,* it's suitable for baking, broiling, grilling and steaming.

Tortilla: Made from corn (called *masa*) or wheat flour, tortillas are thin, flat, round, unleavened Mexican breads that resemble slender pancakes. Traditionally, tortillas are baked, but not browned, on a griddle. They can be eaten plain or wrapped around a multitude of fillings to create tacos, burritos, enchiladas, tostadas and chimichangas. Pick up packaged tortillas in your supermarket's refrigerator section; store them according to package directions.

Vinaigrette: A simple sauce of oil, vinegar and seasonings (herbs, spices, onion and often mustard) used as a salad dressing. The traditional portion of oil to vinegar is 3 to 1, but revamped low-fat versions use less oil. Vinaigrettes also make great marinades for meats, poultry and fish.

Water chestnut: Crisp, white-fleshed and extremely low in fat and calories, water chestnuts are the edible tubers of a water plant from Southeast Asia. They're available fresh in Asian groceries and canned in most supermarkets. Peel fresh water chestnuts before using them.

Watercress: This is a peppery-tasting salad green with small delicate leaves and tender stems. Popular uses include salads, sandwiches and garnishes. Select bunches with healthy-looking stems and dark green leaves. Store in a plastic bag in the refrigerator for up to 2 days.

Whisk: To beat eggs or light liquids with a wire whisk (a kitchen gadget made of looped wires held together by a handle) until blended. A whisk may also be used to blend flour and other dry ingredients.

Wild pecan rice: Also labeled *pecan rice*. Hailing from Louisiana, this delightful aromatic rice has a wonderful nutty flavor. It takes just 20 minutes to cook, and the grains remain fluffy and separate after cooking. Look for it in large supermarkets.

Wine vinegars: These are mildly zesty vinegars made from red or white wines. Use them for marinades, mops, bastes, simple vinaigrettes and other salad dressings.

Worcestershire sauce: A widely available, commercially made, dark, pungent condiment. The exact ingredients in this tasty sauce are a trade secret, but food experts agree that these are the basics: soy sauce, vinegar, garlic, tamarind, onions, molasses, lime and anchovies. Worcestershire sauce was first concocted in India and bottled in Worcestershire, England; hence, its name. It's ideal for perking up many dishes, including marinades, mops, bastes, sauces and, of course, burgers.

Zinfandel: This is a popular, fruity-tasting red wine that can be either robust or light. Also a favorite since the 1980s is white Zinfandel, which is light and fruity.

three/kitchen calculations

You know the routine: A recipe calls for 2 cups broccoli. The supermarket sells fresh broccoli by the pound and the frozen variety in packages. How much should you buy? Another dish requires 2 cups cooked kidney beans. You'd like to use canned. But what size to open? Uncertain and tired of guessing? To help you out, I've listed approximate equivalents (it's impossible to be exact) in this concise list.

Dairy

Butter: 1 stick = $\frac{1}{4}$ pound = 4 ounces = 8 tablespoons

Cheese, blue (or bleu), feta, Gorgonzola: 4 ounces = 1 cup crumbled

Cheese, cheddar, Monterey Jack: 1 pound = 4 cups shredded or grated

Cheese, Parmesan, Romano: 4 ounces = 1 cup shredded or grated

Cream, half & half, sour: $\frac{1}{2}$ pint = 1 cup

Cream cheese: 1 package (3 ounces) = 6 tablespoons; 1 package (8 ounces) = 1 cup

Fruits

Apples: 1 pound = 3 medium = $2\frac{3}{4}$ to 3 cups chopped or sliced

Apricots, dried: 1 pound = $2\frac{3}{4}$ cups = $4\frac{1}{2}$ to $5\frac{1}{2}$ cups cooked

Cranberries: 12-ounce bag whole berries = 3 cups chopped

Cranberries: 1 cup uncooked = 1 cup cooked

Lemon: 1 medium = 2 to 3 teaspoons grated peel and 3 tablespoons juice

Lemons: 1 pound = 4 to 6 medium = 1 cup juice

Lime: 1 medium = 1 teaspoon grated peel and 2 tablespoons juice

Limes: 1 pound = 6 to 8 medium = $\frac{1}{3}$ to $\frac{2}{3}$ cup juice

Mango: 1 medium = 1 cup chopped

Peaches: 1 pound = 3 medium = 2 cups sliced = $1\frac{1}{2}$ cups pulp

Plums: 1 pound = $1\frac{1}{2}$ to 2 cups chopped

Legumes

Beans, kidney, canned: 16 to 17 ounces = 2 cups

Beans, kidney, dried: 1 pound = $2\frac{1}{2}$ cups = $5\frac{1}{2}$ cups cooked

Beans, navy, dried: 1 pound = $2\frac{1}{3}$ cups = $5\frac{1}{2}$ cups cooked

Peas, black-eyed, canned: 16 ounces = 2 cups

Meats

Beef broth: 1 can (14 ounces) = $1\frac{3}{4}$ cups

Beef, cooked, cubed: 1 cup = 6 ounces

Nuts

Almonds, shelled, blanched: $\frac{1}{2}$ pound = $1\frac{1}{2}$ cups whole = 2 cups slivered

Poultry

Chicken, broth: 1 can (14 ounces) = $1\frac{3}{4}$ cups

Chicken, cooked, cubed: 1 cup = 6 ounces

Seasonings

Garlic: 2 medium cloves = 1 teaspoon minced

Herbs, basil, cilantro, dill, parsley, thyme: 1 tablespoon, fresh chopped = 1 teaspoon dried

Onion: 1 medium = $\frac{1}{2}$ cup minced = $\frac{3}{4}$ to 1 cup chopped

Scallions: 2 medium, white part only = 1 tablespoon

Scallions: 2 medium with green tops = $\frac{1}{4}$ cup

Vegetables

Avocado: 1 pound = $2\frac{1}{2}$ cups sliced, diced, or chopped

Beans, green, fresh: 1 pound = $3\frac{1}{2}$ cups whole

Beans, green, frozen: 1 package (9 ounces) = $1\frac{1}{2}$ cups

Beets, fresh, without tops: 1 pound = 2 cups chopped

Broccoli, fresh: 1 pound = 2 cups chopped

Broccoli, frozen: 1 package (10 ounces) = $1\frac{1}{2}$ cups chopped

Brussels sprouts, fresh: 1 pound = 4 cups

Cabbage: 1 pound = $3\frac{1}{2}$ to $4\frac{1}{2}$ cups shredded = 2 cups cooked

Carrots: 1 medium = $\frac{1}{2}$ cup chopped or sliced

Carrots, fresh: 1 pound without tops = 3 cups chopped or sliced = $2\frac{1}{2}$ to 3 cups shredded

Carrots, frozen: 1 package (1 pound) = $2\frac{1}{2}$ to 3 cups sliced

Cauliflower: 1 pound = $1\frac{1}{2}$ cups small florets

Celery: 1 stalk = $\frac{1}{2}$ cup chopped or sliced

Corn, fresh: 2 to 3 ears = 1 cup kernels

Corn, frozen: 1 package (10 ounces) = $1\frac{3}{4}$ cups kernels

Eggplant: 1 pound = 3 to 4 cups diced

Eggplant, uncooked: 1 pound = $\frac{1}{2}$ pound cooked

Mushrooms, fresh: $\frac{1}{2}$ pound = $2\frac{1}{2}$ to 3 cups sliced = 1 cup sautéed

Okra, fresh: 1 pound = 2 cups sliced

Parsnips: 1 pound = 4 medium = 2 cups chopped

Peas, in pod: 1 pound = 1 to $1\frac{1}{2}$ cups shelled

Peas, frozen: 1 package (10 ounces) = 2 cups

Peas, fresh black-eyed: 1 pound = $2\frac{1}{3}$ cups

Peas, frozen black-eyed = 1 package (10 ounces) = $1\frac{1}{2}$ cups

Peas, sugar snap or snow peas: 1 pound = 4 to 5 cups

Peppers, bell: 1 medium = 1 cup chopped

Potatoes, sweet: 1 pound = 3 medium = $3\frac{1}{2}$ to 4 cups cubed or sliced = 2 cups mashed

Potatoes, white: 1 pound = 3 medium = $3\frac{1}{2}$ to 4 cups cubed or sliced = 2 cups mashed

Spinach: 1 pound = 8 to 10 cups torn

Squash, yellow, zucchini: 1 pound = 3 medium = $2\frac{1}{2}$ cups sliced

Squash, winter: 1 pound = 1 cup mashed

Tomato: 1 medium = $\frac{1}{2}$ cup chopped

Tomatoes: 1 pound = 3 large = 4 medium = $1\frac{1}{2}$ cups chopped

Tomatoes: 1 can (28 ounces) crushed = $3\frac{3}{4}$ cups

Turnips: 1 pound = 3 medium

Miscellaneous

Bread: I slice fresh = $\frac{1}{2}$ cup soft crumbs = $\frac{1}{4}$ to $\frac{1}{3}$ cup dry crumbs

Cocoa: $\frac{1}{4}$ pound = 4 ounces = I cup

Cornmeal: I pound dry = 3 cups uncooked = 12 cups cooked

Flour, all purpose: I pound = 3 cups sifted

Flour, whole wheat: I pound = $3\frac{1}{2}$ cups unsifted

Macaroni: I pound = 4 cups dry = 8 cups cooked

Noodles: I pound = 6 cups dry = 7 cups cooked

Rice, brown: I cup uncooked = 4 cups cooked

Rice, white: I cup uncooked = 3 cups cooked

Rice, wild: I cup uncooked = 4 cups cooked

four/measuring up

Need to know how many ounces are in a cup? Or how many milliliters are in a teaspoon? Then check these handy lists of equivalents. Measures are rounded for easy use.

Helpful Measures: U.S. Equivalents

Liquids

I teaspoon = 60 drops = $\frac{1}{6}$ fluid ounce

I tablespoon = 3 teaspoons = $\frac{1}{2}$ fluid ounce

2 tablespoons = $\frac{1}{8}$ cup = I fluid ounce

4 tablespoons = $\frac{1}{4}$ cup = 2 fluid ounces

$5\frac{1}{3}$ tablespoons = $\frac{1}{3}$ cup = $2\frac{1}{2}$ fluid ounces

8 tablespoons = $\frac{1}{2}$ cup = 4 fluid ounces

I cup = 16 tablespoons = 8 fluid ounces

2 cups = I pint = 16 fluid ounces

4 cups = I quart = 32 fluid ounces

4 quarts = I gallon = 128 fluid ounces

Weights

8 ounces = $\frac{1}{2}$ pound

16 ounces = I pound

32 ounces = 2 pounds

36 ounces = $2\frac{1}{4}$ pounds

Helpful Measures: U.S./Metric Equivalents

Liquids

$\frac{1}{4}$ teaspoon = I milliliter

$\frac{1}{2}$ teaspoon = 2 milliliters

I teaspoon = 5 milliliters

I tablespoon = 15 milliliters

I cup = 250 milliliters

2 cups = 500 milliliters

4 cups = I liter

4 quarts = $3\frac{3}{4}$ liters

Weights

I ounce = 28.35 grams

4 ounces = 115 grams

8 ounces = 225 grams

16 ounces = 454 grams

32 ounces = 907 grams

36 ounces = 1000 grams (I kilogram)

Temperatures

32°F = 0°C

212°F = 100°C

five/cooking abbreviations

When you're uncertain about an abbreviation, check it out in this list

t = tsp = teaspoon

T = tbsp = tablespoon

c = cup

oz = ounce

fl oz = fluid ounce

lb = pound

g = gram

k = kilogram

mg = milligram

l = liter

ml = milliliter

F = Fahrenheit

C = Celsius

six/emergency replacements

Fresh out of Italian herb seasoning? Can't locate any herbes de Provence? Don't panic. This list has dozens of quick, easy substitutes that'll work in a pinch. Just be aware that any recipe using a replacement ingredient will have a slightly different taste or texture from the original. Here's how to use the list: Replace the food on the left with the substitute item (in some cases it's a combination of items) to the right of the dash.

Seasonings

Allspice (1 teaspoon) — Cinnamon ($\frac{3}{4}$ teaspoon) and dash of nutmeg

Basil, dried (1 teaspoon) — Italian herb seasoning (1 teaspoon)

Chervil, dried (1 teaspoon) — Tarragon ($\frac{1}{2}$ teaspoon) or parsley ($\frac{1}{2}$ teaspoon)

Chili powder (1 tablespoon) — Hot-pepper sauce (a drop or two) plus oregano ($\frac{1}{4}$ teaspoon) and cumin ($\frac{1}{4}$ teaspoon)

Chinese five-spice powder (1 teaspoon) — Cinnamon ($\frac{1}{4}$ teaspoon), ground red pepper ($\frac{1}{8}$ teaspoon), ground cloves ($\frac{1}{8}$ teaspoon), ground fennel seeds ($\frac{1}{4}$ teaspoon) and ground star anise ($\frac{1}{4}$ teaspoon)

Cilantro (1 teaspoon) — Parsley (1 teaspoon)

Cinnamon (1 teaspoon) — Allspice ($\frac{1}{4}$ teaspoon) or nutmeg ($\frac{1}{4}$ teaspoon)

Cumin (1 teaspoon) — Chili powder (1 teaspoon)

Garlic (1 clove) — Garlic powder ($\frac{1}{8}$ teaspoon) or $\frac{1}{2}$ teaspoon minced garlic in a jar

Ginger (1 teaspoon) — Allspice ($\frac{1}{2}$ teaspoon) or cinnamon (1 teaspoon) or nutmeg ($\frac{1}{2}$ teaspoon)

Herbes de Provence (1 teaspoon) — Rosemary ($\frac{1}{4}$ teaspoon) plus marjoram ($\frac{1}{4}$ teaspoon), thyme ($\frac{1}{4}$ teaspoon) and savory ($\frac{1}{4}$ teaspoon)

Italian herb seasoning (1 teaspoon) — Basil, dried (1 teaspoon) plus thyme, dried leaves (1 teaspoon)

Lemon juice (1 teaspoon) — Cider vinegar ($\frac{1}{2}$ teaspoon) or lime juice (1 teaspoon)

Lemon peel (1 teaspoon grated) — Lemon extract ($\frac{1}{2}$ teaspoon)

Marjoram (1 teaspoon) — Basil (1 teaspoon) or thyme ($\frac{1}{2}$ teaspoon) or savory ($\frac{1}{2}$ teaspoon)

Mustard, dry (1 teaspoon) — Mustard, prepared (1 tablespoon)

Onion (1 minced) — Onions, dried, minced (1 tablespoon)

Oregano, dried (1 teaspoon) — Italian herb seasoning (1 teaspoon)

Poultry seasoning (1 teaspoon) — Thyme ($\frac{1}{4}$ teaspoon) plus sage ($\frac{1}{4}$ teaspoon), rosemary ($\frac{1}{4}$ teaspoon) and nutmeg ($\frac{1}{4}$ teaspoon)

Pumpkin pie spice (1 teaspoon) — Cinnamon, ground (1 teaspoon) plus nutmeg, ground, ($\frac{1}{2}$ teaspoon) and powdered ginger ($\frac{1}{2}$ teaspoon)

Red pepper flakes ($\frac{1}{8}$ teaspoon)—Hot-pepper sauce (dash)

Rosemary ($\frac{1}{2}$ teaspoon) — Thyme ($\frac{1}{2}$ teaspoon) or tarragon ($\frac{1}{2}$ teaspoon) or savory ($\frac{3}{4}$ teaspoon)

Savory (1 teaspoon) — Thyme ($\frac{1}{2}$ teaspoon) or sage ($\frac{1}{2}$ teaspoon)

Sherry (1 tablespoon) — Sherry extract (1 tablespoon)

Tarragon ($\frac{1}{2}$ teaspoon) — Fennel seed (dash) or anise seed (dash)

Teriyaki sauce (1 tablespoon) — Soy sauce (1 tablespoon) plus powdered garlic ($\frac{1}{8}$ teaspoon) and minced fresh ginger ($\frac{1}{4}$ teaspoon)

Thai seasoning (1 teaspoon) — Chili pepper ($\frac{1}{4}$ teaspoon) plus ginger ($\frac{1}{8}$ teaspoon), cumin ($\frac{1}{8}$ teaspoon), cinnamon ($\frac{1}{8}$ teaspoon) and grated lemon peel ($\frac{1}{4}$ teaspoon)

Thyme (1 teaspoon) — Savory (1 teaspoon)

Vinegar (1 teaspoon) — Lemon juice (2 teaspoons)

Thickeners

Cornstarch (1 tablespoon) — All-purpose flour (2 tablespoons)

Flour, as thickener (2 tablespoons) — Cornstarch (1 tablespoon) or quick-cooking tapioca (2 tablespoons)

Instant flour, as thickener (2 tablespoons) — All-purpose flour (2 tablespoons)

Other Ingredients

Bacon (1 slice crumbled) — Bacon bits (1 tablespoon)

Bread crumbs, dry (1 cup) — Cracker crumbs ($\frac{3}{4}$ cup)

Broth, beef or chicken (1 cup) — Bouillon cube (1) plus boiling water (1 cup)

Nonfat sour cream (1 cup) — Plain nonfat yogurt (1 cup)

Parmesan cheese, grated (1 tablespoon) — Romano cheese, grated (1 tablespoon) or provolone cheese, grated (1 tablespoon)

Seasoned bread crumbs, dry (1 cup) — Plain dry bread crumbs ($\frac{7}{8}$ cup) plus grated Parmesan cheese (1 tablespoon) and dried parsley (1 tablespoon)

Tomatoes, canned crushed (1 cup) — Tomatoes, canned diced (1 cup)

Tomatoes, canned sauce (1 cup) — Tomatoes, canned paste ($\frac{1}{2}$ cup) plus water ($\frac{1}{2}$ cup)

Tomatoes, canned whole, cut up (1 cup) — Tomatoes, canned diced (1 cup)

s e v e n / u s i n g   h e r b s   a n d   s p i c e s

A pinch of herb and spice can brighten any grilled dish as well as everyday marinades, mops and bastes. But knowing what seasoning to pair with what food can be confusing, even a little off-putting. To help you find a good match, here are some classic, sure-to-please combinations.

HERBS

Basil: beef, chicken, lamb, salmon, turkey, broccoli, carrots, eggplant, mushrooms, potatoes, summer squash, tomatoes

Bay leaf: beef, chicken, lamb, fish, beets, carrots, potatoes, tomatoes

Chervil: beef, chicken, fish, lamb, shellfish, pork, turkey, asparagus, beets, carrots, eggplant, mushrooms, snowpeas, potatoes, squash, tomatoes

Chives: cheese, potatoes, tomatoes, fish

Cilantro: beef, tomatoes

Dill: chicken, fish, shellfish, cheese, cauliflower, carrots, parsnips, potatoes, tomatoes

Marjoram: beef, chicken, fish, shellfish, lamb, pork, veal, carrots, corn, eggplant, snowpeas, potatoes, summer squash

Mint: chicken, lamb, pork, carrots, snowpeas, potatoes, summer squash, tomatoes

Oregano: beef, chicken, fish, pork, shellfish, turkey, veal, corn, cucumbers, eggplant, mushrooms, potatoes, summer squash, tomatoes

Parsley: beef, chicken, fish, lamb, shellfish, pork, turkey, veal, cheese, cauliflower, corn, eggplant, mushrooms, potatoes, summer squash, tomatoes

Rosemary: beef, chicken, fish, shellfish, lamb, pork, turkey, veal, cauliflower, mushrooms, peas, potatoes, summer squash, tomatoes, turnips

Sage: beef, chicken, flounder, halibut, lamb, pork, veal, beets, Brussels sprouts, carrots, eggplant, snowpeas, potatoes, tomatoes, winter squash

Savory: beef, chicken, fish, lamb, shellfish, turkey, asparagus, carrots, potatoes, tomatoes

Tarragon: beef, chicken, fish, lamb, shellfish, pork, veal, turkey, cheese, asparagus, beets, carrots, cauliflower, mushrooms, potatoes, summer and winter squash, tomatoes

Thyme: beef, chicken, clams, fish, lamb, shellfish, pork, veal, tuna, turkey, cheese, carrots, green beans, potatoes, tomatoes, summer squash

SPICES

Allspice: beef, chicken, fish, ham, turkey, cheese, beets, carrots, parsnips, snowpeas, sweet potatoes, turnips, winter squash

Capers: mixed salad greens

Caraway: beef, pork, onions, potatoes, turnips, winter squash

Cardamom: chicken, fish, cheese, carrots, pumpkin, winter squash, sweet potatoes

Cayenne (red pepper): beef, chicken, fish, shellfish, lamb, pork, turkey, carrots, potatoes, tomatoes.

Celery seed: beef, chicken, fish, lamb, turkey, veal, cheese, beets, cauliflower, potatoes, tomatoes

Cinnamon: beef, chicken, pork, beets, carrots, onions, pumpkin, sweet potatoes, tomatoes, winter squash

Cloves: beef, lamb, pork, beets, carrots, onions, pumpkin, sweet potatoes, winter squash

Coriander: beef, chicken, fish, cauliflower, onions, potatoes, tomatoes

Cumin: beef, chicken, pork, salmon, shellfish, tuna, carrots, tomatoes

Fennel: beef, chicken, lamb, pork, fish, shellfish, onions, snowpeas, summer squash, tomatoes

Gingerroot and ginger: beef, chicken, fish, shellfish, lamb, pork, carrots, summer and winter squash, sweet potatoes

Mace: beef, chicken, shellfish, veal, broccoli, pumpkin, spinach, winter squash

Mustard: beef, chicken, fish, ham, shellfish, pork, beets, Brussels sprouts

Nutmeg: beef, chicken, ham, pork, turkey, corn, eggplant, mushrooms, onions, potatoes, pumpkin, tomatoes, winter squash

Paprika: beef, chicken, turkey, veal, cauliflower, potatoes, turnips

Peppercorns (black with hull, or white without hull): fish, meat, poultry, vegetables

Poppy seed: cabbage, cauliflower, potatoes

Sesame seed: chicken, fish, broccoli, cauliflower, potatoes, tomatoes

Turmeric: beef, chicken, pork, turkey, pumpkin, winter squash

index